CAMBRIDGE LIBRARY COLLECTION

Books of enduring scholarly value

Literary Studies

This series provides a high-quality selection of early printings of literary works, textual editions, anthologies and literary criticism which are of lasting scholarly interest. Ranging from Old English to Shakespeare to early twentieth-century work from around the world, these books offer a valuable resource for scholars in reception history, textual editing, and literary studies.

Literary Blunders

Delight in other people's errors never dates, and this little book, first published in 1893, is a fount of human folly and a joy to read. Its compiler, Henry Benjamin Wheatley (1838–1917), was a distinguished librarian, bibliographer and scholar, and a prolific author on London history and the history of books. This publication displays his great sense of humour, and his effortless command of far-flung sources in the search for a good joke. Citing examples from historians to misguided schoolboys, as well as from everyday conversation, Wheatley looks at comic misprints, misunderstandings, and garbled English in foreign parts. However, the book also has a more serious contribution to make: the chapter on printed errata makes use of the earliest evidence of proof correction by authors, and the analysis of misprints in early printing shows how many variant readings in the works of Shakespeare came about.

Cambridge University Press has long been a pioneer in the reissuing of out-of-print titles from its own backlist, producing digital reprints of books that are still sought after by scholars and students but could not be reprinted economically using traditional technology. The Cambridge Library Collection extends this activity to a wider range of books which are still of importance to researchers and professionals, either for the source material they contain, or as landmarks in the history of their academic discipline.

Drawing from the world-renowned collections in the Cambridge University Library and other partner libraries, and guided by the advice of experts in each subject area, Cambridge University Press is using state-of-the-art scanning machines in its own Printing House to capture the content of each book selected for inclusion. The files are processed to give a consistently clear, crisp image, and the books finished to the high quality standard for which the Press is recognised around the world. The latest print-on-demand technology ensures that the books will remain available indefinitely, and that orders for single or multiple copies can quickly be supplied.

The Cambridge Library Collection brings back to life books of enduring scholarly value (including out-of-copyright works originally issued by other publishers) across a wide range of disciplines in the humanities and social sciences and in science and technology.

Literary Blunders

A Chapter in the History of Human Error

Henry Benjamin Wheatley

CAMBRIDGE UNIVERSITY PRESS

Cambridge, New York, Melbourne, Madrid, Cape Town,
Singapore, São Paolo, Delhi, Mexico City

Published in the United States of America by Cambridge University Press, New York

www.cambridge.org
Information on this title: www.cambridge.org/9781108051996

© in this compilation Cambridge University Press 2012

This edition first published 1893
This digitally printed version 2012

ISBN 978-1-108-05199-6 Paperback

The Book-Lover's Library

Edited by

Henry B. Wheatley, F.S.A.

LITERARY BLUNDERS

A CHAPTER IN THE

"HISTORY OF HUMAN ERROR"

BY

HENRY B. WHEATLEY, F.S.A.

LONDON

ELLIOT STOCK, 62, PATERNOSTER ROW

1893

PREFACE.

EVERY *reader of* The Caxtons *will remember the description, in that charming novel, of the gradual growth of Augustine Caxton's great work "The History of Human Error," and how, in fact, the existence of that work forms the pivot round which the incidents turn. It was modestly expected to extend to five quarto volumes, but only the first seven sheets were printed by Uncle Jack's Anti-Publishers' Society, "with sundry unfinished plates depicting the various developments of the human skull (that temple of Human Error)," and the remainder has not been heard of since.*

In introducing to the reader a small branch of this inexhaustible subject, I have ventured to make use of Augustine Caxton's title; but I trust that no one will allow himself to imagine that I intend, in the future, to produce the thousand or so volumes which will be required to complete the work.

A satirical friend who has seen the proofs of this little volume says it should be entitled "Jokes Old and New"; but I find that he seldom acknowledges that a joke is new, and I hope, therefore, my readers will transpose the adjectives, and accept the old jokes for the sake of the new ones. I may claim, at least, that the series of answers to examination questions, which Prof. Oliver Lodge has so kindly supplied me with, comes within the latter class.

I trust that if some parts of the book are thought to be frivolous, the chapters on lists of errata and misprints may be found to contain some useful literary information.

I have availed myself of the published communications of my friends Professors Hales and Skeat and Dr. Murray on Literary Blunders, and my best thanks are also due to several friends who have helped me with some curious instances, and I would specially mention Sir George Birdwood, K.C.I.E., C.S.I., Mr. Edward Clodd, Mr. R. B. Prosser, and Sir Henry Trueman Wood.

CONTENTS.

CHAPTER I.

BLUNDERS IN GENERAL.

CHAPTER II.

BLUNDERS OF AUTHORS.

LITERARY BLUNDERS.

CHAPTER I.

BLUNDERS IN GENERAL.

HE words " blunder " and " mistake " are often treated as synonyms ; thus we usually call our own blunders mistakes, and our friends style our mistakes blunders. In truth the class of blunders is a subdivision of the *genus* mistakes. Many mistakes are very serious in their consequences, but there is almost always some sense of fun connected with a blunder, which is a mistake usually caused by some mental confusion. Lexicographers state that it is an error due to stupidity and carelessness, but blunders are often caused

1

by a too great sharpness and quickness. Sometimes a blunder is no mistake at all, as when a man blunders on the right explanation; thus he arrives at the right goal, but by an unorthodox road. Sir Roger L'Estrange says that " it is one thing to forget a matter of fact, and another to *blunder* upon the reason of it."

Some years ago there was an article in the *Saturday Review* on " the knowledge necessary to make a blunder," and this title gives the clue to what a blunder really is. It is caused by a confusion of two or more things, and unless something is known of these things a blunder cannot be made. A perfectly ignorant man has not sufficient knowledge to make a blunder.

An ordinary blunder may die, and do no great harm, but a literary blunder often has an extraordinary life. Of literary blunders probably the philological are the most persistent and the most difficult to kill. In this class may be mentioned (1) Ghost words, as they are called by Professor Skeat—words, that is, which have been registered, but which never really existed; (2) Real words that exist through a mistake ; and (3) Absurd etymologies, a large division crammed with delicious blunders.

1. Professor Skeat, in his presidential address to the members of the Philological Society in 1886, gave a most interesting account of some hundred ghost words, or words which have no real existence. Those who wish to follow out this subject must refer to the *Philological Transactions*, but four specially curious instances may be mentioned here. These four words are " abacot," "knise," "morse," and " polien." *Abacot* is defined by Webster as " the cap of state formerly used by English kings, wrought into the figure of two crowns " ; but Dr. Murray, when he was preparing the *New English Dictionary*, discovered that this was an interloper, and unworthy of a place in the language. It was found to be a mistake for *by-cocket*, which is the correct word. In spite of this exposure of the impostor, the word was allowed to stand, with a woodcut of an abacot, in an important dictionary published subsequently, although Dr. Murray's remarks were quoted. This shows how difficult it is to kill a word which has

once found shelter in our dictionaries. *Knise* is a charming word which first appeared in a number of the *Edinburgh Review* in 1808. Fortunately for the fun of the thing, the word occurred in an article on Indian Missions, by Sydney Smith. We read, "The Hindoos have some very strange customs, which it would be desirable to abolish. Some swing on hooks, some run *knises* through their hands, and widows burn themselves to death." The reviewer was attacked for his statement by Mr. John Styles, and he replied in an article on Methodism printed in the *Edinburgh* in the following year. Sydney Smith wrote : " Mr. Styles is peculiarly severe upon us for not being more shocked at their piercing their limbs with *knises* . . . it is for us to explain the plan and nature of this terrible and unknown piece of mechanism. A *knise*, then, is neither more nor less than a false print in the *Edinburgh Review* for a knife ; and from this blunder of the printer has Mr. Styles manufactured this Dædalean instrument of torture called a *knise*." A similar instance occurs in a misprint of a passage

of one of Scott's novels, but here there is
the further amusing circumstance that the
etymology of the false word was settled to
the satisfaction of some of the readers. In
the majority of editions of *The Monastery*,
chapter x., we read : " Hardened wretch
(said Father Eustace), art thou but this
instant delivered from death, and dost thou
so soon *morse* thoughts of slaughter ? "
This word is nothing but a misprint of
nurse ; but in *Notes and Queries* two independent correspondents accounted for the
word *morse* etymologically. One explained
it as " to prime," as when one primes a
musket, from O. Fr. *amorce*, powder for the
touchhole (Cotgrave), and the other by " to
bite " (Lat. *mordere*), hence " to indulge
in biting, stinging or gnawing thoughts of
slaughter." The latter writes : " That the
word as a misprint should have been
printed and read by millions for fifty
years without being challenged and altered
exceeds the bounds of probability." Yet
when the original MS. of Sir Walter Scott
was consulted, it was found that the word
was there plainly written *nurse*.

The Saxon letter for *th* (þ) has long

been a sore puzzle to the uninitiated, and
it came to be represented by the letter *y*.
Most of those who think they are writing
in a specially archaic manner when they
spell "ye" for "the" are ignorant of this,
and pronounce the article as if it were the
pronoun. Dr. Skeat quotes a curious instance of the misreading of the thorn (þ)
as *p*, by which a strange ghost word is
evolved. Whitaker, in his edition of Piers
Plowman, reads that Christ "*polede* for
man," which should be *tholede*, from
tholien, to suffer, as there is no such
verb as *polien*.

Dr. J. A. H. Murray, the learned editor
of the Philological Society's *New English
Dictionary*, quotes two amusing instances
of ghost words in a communication to
Notes and Queries (7th S., vii. 305). He
says: "Possessors of Jamieson's Scottish
Dictionary will do well to strike out the
fictitious entry *cietezour*, cited from Bellenden's *Chronicle* in the plural *cietezouris*,
which is merely a misreading of cietezanis
(*i.e.* with Scottish z = ȝ = y), *cieteyanis* or
citeyanis, Bellenden's regular word for
citizens. One regrets to see this absurd

mistake copied from Jamieson (unfortunately without acknowledgment) by the compilers of Cassell's *Encyclopædic Dictionary.*"

"Some editions of Drayton's *Barons Wars*, Bk. VI., st. xxxvii., read—

"'And ciffy Cynthus with a thousand birds,'

which nonsense is solemnly reproduced in Campbell's *Specimens of the British Poets*, iii. 16. It may save some readers a needless reference to the dictionary to remember that it is a misprint for cliffy, a favourite word of Drayton's."

2. In contrast to supposed words that never did exist, are real words that exist through a mistake, such as *apron* and *adder*, where the *n*, which really belongs to the word itself, has been supposed, mistakenly, to belong to the article ; thus apron should be napron (Fr. *naperon*), and adder should be nadder (A.-S. *næddre*). An amusing confusion has arisen in respect to the Ridings of Yorkshire, of which there are three. The word should be *triding*, but the *t* has got lost in the adjective, as West Triding became West Riding. The origin of

the word has thus been quite lost sight of, and at the first organisation of the Province of Upper Canada, in 1798, the county of Lincoln was divided into *four* ridings and the county of York into *two.* York was afterwards supplied with *four.*

Sir Henry Bennet, in the reign of Charles II., took his title of Earl of Arlington owing to a blunder. The proper name of the village in Middlesex is Harlington.

A curious misunderstanding in the Marriage Service has given us two words instead of one. We now vow to remain united till death us *do part,* but the original declaration, as given in the first Prayer Book of Edward VI., was : " I, N., take thee N., to my wedded wife, to have and to hold from this day forward, for better, for worse, for richer, for poorer, in sickness and in health, to love and to cherish, till death us depart [or separate]."

It is not worth while here to register the many words which have taken their present spelling through a mistaken view of their etymology. They are too numerous, and the consideration of them would open up a question quite distinct from the one now under consideration.

3. Absurd etymology was once the rule, because guessing without any knowledge of the historical forms of words was general; and still, in spite of the modern school of philology, which has shown us the right way, much wild guessing continues to be prevalent. It is not, however, often that we can point to such a brilliant instance of blundering etymology as that to be found in Barlow's English Dictionary (1772). The word *porcelain* is there said to be "derived from *pour cent annes*, French for a hundred years, it having been imagined that the materials were matured underground for that term of years."

Richardson, the novelist, suggests an etymology almost equal to this. He writes, "What does correspondence mean? It is a word of Latin origin : a compound word; and the two elements here brought together are *respondeo*, I answer, and *cor*, the heart : *i.e.*, I answer feelingly, I reply not so much to the head as to the heart."

Dr. Ash's English Dictionary, published in 1775, is an exceedingly useful work, as containing many words and forms of words nowhere else registered, but it contains some curious mistakes. The chief and best-known one is the explanation of the word *curmudgeon*—" from the French *cœur*, unknown, and *mechant*, a correspondent." The only explanation of this absurdly confused etymology is that an ignorant man was employed to copy from Johnson's Dictionary, where the authority was given as "an unknown correspondent," and he, supposing these words to be a translation of the French, set them down as such. The two words *esoteric* and *exoteric* were not so frequently used in the last century as they are now; so perhaps there may be some excuse for the following entry: "Esoteric (adj. an incorrect spelling) exoteric." Dr. Ash could not have been well read in Arthurian literature, or he would not have turned the noble knight Sir Gawaine into a woman, " the sister of King Arthur." There is a story of a blunder in Littleton's Latin Dictionary, which further research has proved to be no mistake at all. It is said that when the Doctor was compiling his work, and

announced the word *concurro* to his
amanuensis, the scribe, imagining from the
sound that the six first letters would give
the translation of the verb, said "Concur,
sir, I suppose?" to which the Doctor
peevishly replied, "Concur—condog!"
and in the edition of 1678 "condog" is
printed as one interpretation of *concurro.*
Now, an answer to this story is that, however odd a word "condog" may appear,
it will be found in Henry Cockeram's
English Dictionarie, first published in
1623. The entry is as follows : "to agree,
concurre, cohere, condog, condiscend."

Mistakes are frequently made in respect
of foreign words which retain their original
form, especially those which retain their
Latin plurals, the feminine singular being
often confused with the neuter plural. For
instance, there is the word *animalcule*
(plural *animalcules*), also written *animal-
culum* (plural *animalcula*). Now, the
plural *animalcula* is often supposed to be
the feminine singular, and a new plural is
at once made—*animalculæ*. This blunder
is one constantly being made, while it is
only occasionally we see a supposed plural

stratæ in geology from a supposed singular
strata, and the supposed singular *formulum*
from a supposed plural *formula* will probably turn up some day.

In connection with popular etymology,
it seems proper to make a passing mention
of the sailors' perversion of the Bellero-
phon into the Billy Ruffian, the Hiron-
delle into the Iron Devil, and La Bonne
Corvette into the Bonny Cravat. Some
of the supposed changes in public-house
signs, such as Bull and Mouth from
" Boulogne mouth," and Goat and Com-
passes from " God encompasseth us," are
more than doubtful ; but the Bacchanals
has certainly changed into the Bag o' nails,
and the George Canning into the George
and Cannon. The words in the language
that have been formed from a false analogy
are so numerous and have so often been
noted that we must not allow them to
detain us here longer.

Imaginary persons have been brought
into being owing to blundering misreading. For instance, there are many saints
in the Roman calendar whose individu-
ality it would not be easy to prove. All

know how St. Veronica came into being, and equally well known is the origin of St. Ursula and her eleven thousand virgins. In this case, through the misreading of her name, the unfortunate virgin martyr Undecimilla has dropped out of the calendar.

Less known is the origin of Saint Xynoris, the martyr of Antioch, who is noticed in the *Martyrologie Romaine* of Baronius. Her name was obtained by a misreading of Chrysostom, who, referring to two martyrs, uses the word ξυνωρὶς (couple or pair).

In the City of London there is a church dedicated to St. Vedast, which is situated in Foster Lane, and is often described as St. Vedast, *alias* Foster. This has puzzled many, and James Paterson, in his *Pietas Londinensis* (1714), hazarded the opinion that the church was dedicated to "two conjunct saints." He writes: "At the first it was called St. Foster's in memory of some founder or ancient benefactor, but afterwards it was dedicated to St. Vedast, Bishop of Arras." Newcourt makes a similar mistake in his *Reper-*

torium, but Thomas Fuller knew the
truth, and in his *Church History* refers to
" St. Vedastus, *anglice* St. Fosters." This
is the fact, and the name St. Fauster or
Foster is nothing more than a corruption
of St. Vedast, all the steps of which we
now know. My friend Mr. Danby P. Fry
worked this out some years ago, but his
difficulty rested with the second syllable
of the name Foster; but the links in the
chain of evidence have been completed
by reference to Mr. H. C. Maxwell Lyte's
valuable Report on the Manuscripts of the
Dean and Chapter of St. Paul's. The
first stage in the corruption took place in
France, and the name must have been
introduced into this country as Vast.
This loss of the middle consonant is in
accordance with the constant practice in
early French of dropping out the consonant preceding an accented vowel, as
reine from *regina.* The change of
Augustine to *Austin* is an analogous
instance. *Vast* would here be pronounced
Vaust, in the same way as the word *vase*
is still sometimes pronounced *vause.* The
interchange of *v* and *f,* as in the cases of

Vane and *Fane* and *fox* and *vixen*, is too common to need more than a passing notice. We have now arrived at the form St. Faust, and the evidence of the old deeds of St. Paul's explains the rest, showing us that the second syllable has grown out of the possessive case. In one of 8 Edward III. we read of the " King's highway, called Seint Fastes lane." Of course this was pronounced *St. Faustés,* and we at once have the two syllables. The next form is in a deed of May 1360, where it stands as " Seyn Fastreslane." We have here, not a final *r* as in the latest form, but merely an intrusive trill. This follows the rule by which *thesaurus* became *treasure, Hebudas, Hebrides,* and *culpatus, culprit.* After the great Fire of London, the church was re-named St. Vedast (*alias* Foster)—a form of the name which it had never borne before, except in Latin deeds as Vedastus.[1] More might be said

---

[1] See an article by the Author in *The Athenæum,* January 3rd, 1885, p. 15 ; and a paper by the Rev. W. Sparrow Simpson in the *Journal of the British Archæological Association* (vol. xliii., p. 56).

of the corruptions of names in the cases
of other saints, but these corruptions are
more the cause of blunders in others than
blunders in themselves.   It is not often
that a new saint is evolved with such an
English name as Foster.

The existence of the famous St. Vitus
has been doubted, and his dance (*Chorea
Sancti Vitæ*) is supposed to have been
originally *chorea invita*.   But the strangest
of saints was S. Viar, who is thus accounted
for by D'Israeli in his *Curiosities of
Literature* :—

"Mabillon has preserved a curious
literary blunder of some pious Spaniards
who applied to the Pope for consecrating a
day in honour of Saint Viar.   His Holiness
in the voluminous catalogue of his saints
was ignorant of this one.   The only proof
brought forward for his existence was this
inscription :—

S. VIAR.

An antiquary, however, hindered one more
festival in the Catholic calendar by con-
vincing them that these letters were only
the remains of an inscription erected for

an ancient surveyor of the roads ; and he
read their saintship thus :—

[PREFECTV]S VIAR[VM]."

Foreign travellers in England have
usually made sad havoc of the names of
places. Hentzner spelt Gray's Inn and
Lincoln's Inn phonetically as Grezin and
Linconsin, and so puzzled his editor that he
supposed these to be the names of two
giants. A similar mistake to this was that
of the man who boasted that "not all the
British House of Commons, not the whole
bench of Bishops, not even Leviticus himself, should prevent him from marrying his
deceased wife's sister." One of the jokes
in Mark Twain's *Huckleberry Finn*
(ch. xxiii.) turns on the use of this same
expression "Leviticus himself."

The picturesque writer who draws a
well-filled-in picture from insufficient data
is peculiarly liable to fall into blunders,
and when he does fall it is not surprising
that less imaginative writers should
chuckle over his fall. A few years ago
an American editor is said to have received the telegram " Oxford Music Hall

burned to the ground." There was not
much information here, and he was ignorant of the fact that this building was in
London and in Oxford Street, but he was
equal to the occasion. He elaborated a
remarkable account of the destruction
by fire of the principal music hall of
academic Oxford. He told how it was
situated in the midst of historic colleges
which had miraculously escaped destruction by the flames. These flames, fanned
into a fury by a favourable wind, lit up
the academic spires and groves as they
ran along the rich cornices, lapped the
gorgeous pillars, shrivelled up the roof
and grasped the mighty walls of the
ancient building in their destructive
embraces.

In 1882 an announcement was made
in a weekly paper that some prehistoric
remains had been found near the Church
of San Francisco, Florence. The note
was reproduced in an evening paper and
in an antiquarian monthly with words in
both cases implying that the locality of
the find was San Francisco, California.

It is a common mistake of those who

have heard of Grolier bindings to suppose
that the eminent book collector was a
binder; but this is nothing to that of the
workman who told the writer of this that
he had found out the secret of making
the famous Henri II. or Oiron ware. "In
fact," he added, " I could make it as well
as Henry Deux himself." The idea of the
king of France working in the potteries
is exceedingly fine.

Family pride is sometimes the cause
of exceedingly foolish blunders. The
following amusing passage in Anderson's
Genealogical History of the House of Yvery
(1742) illustrates a form of pride ridiculed
by Lord Chesterfield when he set up on
his walls the portraits of Adam de Stanhope
and Eve de Stanhope. The having a
stutterer in the family will appear to most
readers to be a strange cause of pride.
The author writes : " It was usual in ancient
times with the greatest families, and is by
all genealogists allowed to be a mighty evidence of dignity, to use certain nicknames,
which the French call sobriquets . . .
such as 'the Lame' or 'the Black.' . . .
The house of Yvery, not deficient in any

mark or proof of greatness and antiquity,
abounds at different periods in instances
of this nature.   Roger, a younger son of
William Youel de Perceval, was surnamed
Balbus or the Stutterer."

Sometimes a blunder has turned out
fortunate in its consequences ; and a
striking instance of this is recorded in the
history of Prussia.   Frederic I. charged
his ambassador Bartholdi with the mission
of procuring from the Emperor of Germany an acknowledgment of the regal
dignity which he had just assumed.   It
is said that instructions written in cypher
were sent to him, with particular directions
that he should not apply on this subject
to Father Wolff, the Emperor's confessor.
The person who copied these instructions,
however, happened to omit the word *not*
in the copy in cypher.   Bartholdi was
surprised at the order, but obeyed it and
made the matter known to Wolff; who,
in the greatest astonishment, declared that
although he had always been hostile to
the measure, he could not resist this
proof of the Elector's confidence, which
had made a deep impression upon him.

It was thought that the mediation of the confessor had much to do with the accomplishment of the Elector's wishes.

Misquotations form a branch of literary blunders which may be mentioned here. The text " He may run that readeth it " (Hab. ii. 2) is almost invariably quoted as " He who runs may read "; and the Divine condemnation " In the sweat of thy face shalt thou eat bread " (Gen. iii. 19) is usually quoted as " sweat of thy brow."

The manner in which Dr. Johnson selected the quotations for his Dictionary is well known, and as a general rule these are tolerably accurate; but under the thirteenth heading of the verb to sit will be found a curious perversion of a text of Scripture. There we read, " Asses are ye that sit in judgement— *Judges*," but of course there is no such passage in the Bible. The correct reading of the tenth verse of the fifth chapter is : " Speak, ye that ride on white asses, ye that sit in judgment, and walk by the way."

From misquotations it is an easy step

to pass to mispronunciations. These are
mostly too common to be amusing, but
sometimes the blunderers manage to hit
upon something which is rather comic.
Thus an ignorant reader coming upon a
reference to an angle of forty-five degrees
was puzzled, and astonished his hearers
by giving it out as *angel* of forty-five
degrees. This blunderer, however, was
outdone by the speaker who described a
distinguished personage " as a very inde-
fatēgable young man," adding, " but even
he must succumb " (suck 'um) at last.

As has already been said, blunders are
often made by those who are what we
usually call " too clever by half." Surely
it was a blunder to change the time-
honoured name of King's Bench to
Queen's Bench. A queen is a female
king, and she reigns as a king; the
absurdity of the change of sex in the
description is more clearly seen when
we find in a Prayer-book published soon
after the Queen's accession Her Majesty
described as "our Queen and *Governess*."

Editors of classical authors are often
laughed at for their emendations, but

sometimes unjustly. When we consider
the crop of blunders that have gathered
about the texts of celebrated books, we
shåll be grateful for the labours of brilliant
scholars who have cleared these away
and made obscure passages intelligible.

One of the most remarkable emendations ever made by an editor is that of
Theobald in Mrs. Quickly's description of
Falstaff's deathbed (*King Henry V.*, act ii.,
sc. 4). The original is unintelligible :
" his nose was as sharp as a pen and a
table of greene fields." A friend suggested
that it should read "'a talked," and Theobald then suggested "'a babbled," a reading
which has found its way into all texts,
and is never likely to be ousted from its
place. Collier's MS. corrector turned the
sentence into " as a pen on a table of
green frieze." Very few who quote this
passage from Shakespeare have any notion
of how much they owe to Theobald.

Sometimes blunders are intentionally
made—malapropisms which are understood by the speaker's intimates, but often
astonish strangers—such as the expressions
" the sinecure of every eye," " as white

as the drivelling snow." [1]   Of intentional
mistakes, the best known are those which
have been called cross readings, in which
the reader is supposed to read across the
page instead of down the column of a
newspaper, with such results as the following :—

"A new Bank was lately opened at
Northampton—☞ no money returned."

"The Speaker's public dinners will
commence next week—admittance, 3/- to
see the animals fed."

As blunders are a class of mistakes, so
"bulls" are a sub-class of blunders.   No
satisfactory explanation of the word has
been given, although it appears to be
intimately connected with the word
blunder.   Equally the thing itself has not
been very accurately defined.

The author of *A New Booke of Mistakes*, 1637, which treats of "Quips,
Taunts, Retorts, Flowts, Frumps, Mockes,
Gibes, Jestes, etc.," says in his address to
the Reader, "There are moreover other
simple mistakes in speech which pass

[1] See *Spectator*, December 24th, 1887, for
specimens of family lingo.

under the name of Bulls, but if any man shall demand of mee why they be so called, I must put them off with this woman's reason, they are so because they bee so." All the author can affirm is that they have no connection with the inns and playhouses of his time styled the Black Bulls and the Red Bulls. Coleridge's definition is the best: "A bull consists in a mental juxtaposition of incongruous ideas with the sensation but without the sense of connection." [1]

Bulls are usually associated with the Irish, but most other nations are quite capable of making them, and Swift is said to have intended to write an essay on English bulls and blunders. Sir Thomas Trevor, a Baron of the Exchequer 1625-49, when presiding at the Bury Assizes, had a cause about wintering of cattle before him. He thought the charge immoderate, and said, "Why, friend, this is most unreasonable ; I wonder thou art not ashamed, for I myself have known a beast wintered one whole summer for a noble." The man at

[1] Southey's *Omniana*, vol. i., p. 220.

once, with ready wit, cried, "That was a
bull, my lord." Whereat the company
was highly amused.[1]

One of the best-known bulls is that inscribed on the obelisk near Fort William
in the Highlands of Scotland. In this
inscription a very clumsy attempt is made
to distinguish between natural tracks and
made roads :—

> " Had you seen these roads before they
>   were made,
>   You would lift up your hands and bless
>   General Wade."

The bulletins of Pope Clement XIV.'s
last illness, which were announced at the
Vatican, culminated in a very fair bull.
The notices commenced with " His Holi-
ness is very ill," and ended with " His
Infallibility is delirious."

Negro bulls have frequently been reported, but the health once proposed by
a worthy black is perhaps as good an
instance as could be cited. He pledged
" De Gobernor ob our State ! He come

[1] Thoms, *Anecdotes and Traditions,* 1839, p
79.

in wid much opposition; he go out wid
none at all."

Still, in spite of the fact that all nations
fall into these blunders, and that, as it
has been said of some, *Hibernicis ipsis
Hibernior*, it is to Ireland that we look
for the finest examples of bulls, and we
do not usually look in vain.

It is in a Belfast paper that may be
read the account of a murder, the result
of which is described thus : " They fired
two shots at him; the first shot killed
him, but the second was not fatal." Con-
noisseurs in bulls will probably say that
this is only a blunder. Perhaps the following will please them better : " A man
was run down by a passenger train and
killed ; he was injured in a similar way a
year ago."

Here are three good bulls, which fulfil
all the conditions we expect in this branch
of wit. We know what the writer means,
although he does not exactly say it. This
passage is from the report of an Irish
Benevolent Society : " Notwithstanding
the large amount paid for medicine and
medical attendance, very few deaths

occurred during the year." A country
editor's correspondent wrote : "Will you
please to insert this obituary notice ? I
make bold to ask it, because I know the
deceased had a great many friends who
would be glad to hear of his death." The
third is quoted in the *Greville Memoirs* :
"He abjured the errors of the Romish
Church, and embraced those of the
Protestant."

It is said that the Irish Statute Book
opens characteristically with, "An Act
that the King's officers may travel *by sea*
from one place to another within the *land*
of Ireland "; but one of the main objects
of the *Essay on Irish Bulls*, by Maria
Edgeworth and her father, Richard Lovell
Edgeworth, was to show that the title of
their work was incorrect. They find the
original of Paddy Blake's echo in Bacon's
works : "I remember well that when I
went to the echo at Port Charenton, there
was an old Parisian that took it to be the
work of spirits, and of good spirits ; ' for,'
said he, ' call Satan, and the echo will not
deliver back the devil's name, but will
say, "Va-t'en."'" Mr. Hill Burton found

the original of Sir Boyle Roche's bull of
the bird which was in two places at once
in a letter of a Scotsman—Robertson of
Rowan. Steele said that all was the effect
of climate, and that, if an Englishman were
born in Ireland, he would make as many
bulls. Mistakes of an equally absurd
character may be found in English Acts
of Parliament, such as this : " The new
gaol to be built from the materials of
the old one, and the prisoners to remain
in the latter till the former is ready " ; or
the disposition of the prisoner's punishment of transportation for seven years—
"half to go to the king, and the other half
to the informer." Peter Harrison, an an-
notator on the Pentateuch, observed of
Moses' two *tables of stone* that they were
made of *shittim wood*. This is not unlike
the title said to have been used for a useful
little work—" Every man his own Washer-
woman." Horace Walpole said that the
best of all bulls was that of the man who,
complaining of his nurse, said, " I hate
that woman, for she changed me at
nurse." But surely this one quoted by
Mr. Hill Burton is far superior to Horace

Walpole's; in fact, one of the best ever conceived. Result of a duel—" The one party received a slight wound in the breast; the other fired in the air—and so the matter terminated."

After this the description of the wrongs of Ireland has a somewhat artificial look : " Her cup of misery has been overflowing, and is not yet full."

CHAPTER II.

Blunders of Authors.

ACAULAY, in his life of Goldsmith in the *Encyclopædia Britannica*, relates that that author, in the *History of England*, tells us that Naseby is in Yorkshire, and that the mistake was not corrected when the book was reprinted. He further affirms that Goldsmith was nearly hoaxed into putting into the *History of Greece* an account of a battle between Alexander the Great and Montezuma. This, however, is scarcely a fair charge, for the backs of most of us need to be broad enough to bear the actual blunders we have made throughout life without having to bear those which we almost made.

Goldsmith was a very remarkable instance of a man who undertook to write books on subjects of which he knew nothing. Thus, Johnson said that if he could tell a horse from a cow that was the extent of his knowledge of zoology ; and yet the *History of Animated Nature* can still be read with pleasure from the charm of the author's style.

Some authors are so careless in the construction of their works as to contradict in one part what they have already stated in another. In the year 1828 an amusing work was published on the clubs of London, which contained a chapter on Fighting Fitzgerald, of whom the author writes : " That Mr. Fitzgerald (unlike his countrymen generally) was totally devoid of generosity, no one who ever knew him will doubt." In another chapter on the same person the author flatly contradicts his own judgment : " In summing up the catalogue of his vices, however, we ought not to shut our eyes upon his virtues ; of the latter, he certainly possessed that one for which his countrymen have always been so famous, generosity." The scissors-and-paste compilers are peculiarly liable to such errors as these ; and a writer in the *Quarterly Review* proved the *Mémoires de Louis XVIII.* (published in 1832) to be a mendacious compilation from the *Mémoires de Bachaumont* by giving examples of the compiler's blundering. One of these muddles is well worth quoting, and it occurs in the following passage : "Seven bishops—of *Puy*, Gallard de Terraube ; of *Langres*, La Luzerne ; of *Rhodez*, Seignelay-Colbert; of *Gast*, Le Tria ; of *Blois*, Laussiere Themines ; of *Nancy*, Fontanges ; of *Alais*, Beausset ; of *Nevers*, Seguiran." Had the compiler taken the trouble to count his own list, he would have seen that he had given eight names instead of seven, and so have suspected that something was wrong ; but he was not paid to think. The fact is that there is no such place as Gast, and there was no such person as Le Tria. The Bishop of Rhodez was Seignelay-Colbert de Castle Hill, a descendant of the Scotch family of Cuthbert of Castle Hill, in Inverness-shire ; and Bachaumont misled his successor by writing Gast Le Hill for Castle Hill. The introduction of a stop and a little more misspelling resulted in the blunder as we now find it.

3

Authors and editors are very apt to take things for granted, and they thus fall into errors which might have been escaped if they had made inquiries. Pope, in a note on *Measure for Measure*, informs us that the story was taken from Cinthio's novel *Dec.* 8 *Nov.* 5, thus contracting the words decade and novel. Warburton, in his edition of Shakespeare, was misled by these contractions, and fills them up as December 8 and November 5. Many blunders are merely clerical errors of the authors, who are led into them by a curious association of ideas ; thus, in the *Lives of the Londonderrys*, Sir Archibald Alison, when describing the funeral of the Duke of Wellington in St. Paul's, speaks of one of the pall-bearers as Sir Peregrine Pickle, instead of Sir Peregrine Maitland. Dickens, in *Bleak House*, calls Harold Skimpole Leonard throughout an entire number, but returns to the old name in a subsequent one.

Few authors require to be more on their guard against mistakes than historians, especially as they are peculiarly liable to fall into them. What shall we think of the authority of a school book when we find the statement that Louis Napoleon was Consul in 1853 before he became Emperor of the French?

We must now pass from a book of small value to an important work on the history of England ; but it will be necessary first to make a few explanatory remarks. Our readers know that English kings for several centuries claimed the power of curing scrofula, or king's evil; but they may not be so well acquainted with the fact that the French sovereigns were believed to enjoy the same miraculous power. Such, however, was the case ; and tradition reported that a phial filled with holy oil was sent down from heaven to be used for the anointing of the kings at their coronation. We can illustrate this by an anecdote of Napoleon. Lafayette and the first Consul had a conversation one day on the government of the United States. Bonaparte did not agree with Lafayette's views, and the latter told him that "he was desirous of having the ittle phial broke over his head." This *sainte ampulle,* or holy vessel, was an important object in the ceremony, and the virtue of the oil was to confer the power of cure upon the anointed king. This the historian could not have known, or he would not have written: "The French were confident in themselves, in their fortunes; in the special gifts by which they held the stars." If this were all the information that was given us, we should be left in a perfect state of bewilderment while trying to understand how the French could hold the stars, or, if they were able to hold them, what good it would do them; but the historian adds a note which, although it contains some new blunders, gives the clue to an explanation of an otherwise inexplicable passage. It is as follows: "The Cardinal of Lorraine showed Sir William Pickering the precious ointment of St. Ampull, wherewith the King of France was sacred, which he said was sent from heaven above a thousand years ago, and since by miracle preserved, through whose virtue also the king held *les estroilles.*" From this we might imagine that the holy Ampulla was a person; but the clue to the whole confusion is to be found in the last word of the sentence. As the French language does not contain any such word as *estroilles*, there can be no doubt that it stands for old French *escroilles*, or the king's evil. The change of a few letters has here made the mighty difference between the power of curing scrofula and the gift of holding the stars.

In some copies of John Britton's *Descriptive Sketches of Tunbridge Wells* (1832) the following extraordinary passage will be found : "Judge Jefferies, a man who has rendered his name infamous in the annals of history by the cruelty and injustice he manifested in presiding at the trial of King Charles I." The book was no sooner issued than the author became aware of his astonishing chronological blunder, and he did all in his power to set the matter right; but a mistake in print can never be entirely obliterated. However much trouble may be taken to suppress a book, some copies will be sure to escape, and, becoming valuable by the attempted suppression, attract all the more attention.

Scott makes David Ramsay, in the

Fortunes of Nigel (chapter ii.), swear "by the bones of the immortal Napier." It would perhaps be rank heresy to suppose that Sir Walter did not know that "Napier's bones" were an apparatus for purposes of calculation, but he certainly puts the expression in such an ambiguous form that many of his readers are likely to suppose that the actual bones of Napier's body were intended.

Some of the most curious of blunders are those made by learned men who without thought set down something which at another time they would recognise as a mistake. The following passage from Mr. Gladstone's *Gleanings of Past Years* (vol. i., p. 26), in which the author confuses Daniel with Shadrach, Meshech, and Abednego, has been pointed out : "The fierce light that beats upon a throne is sometimes like the heat of that furnace in which only Daniel could walk unscathed, too fierce for those whose place it is to stand in its vicinity." Who would expect to find Macaulay blundering on a subject he knew so well as the story of the *Faerie Queene*! and yet this is what he wrote in a review of Southey's edition of the *Pilgrim's Progress*: "Nay, even Spenser himself, though assuredly one of the greatest poets that ever lived, could not succeed in the attempt to make allegory interesting. . . . One unpardonable fault, the fault of tediousness, pervades the whole of the *Fairy Queen*. We become sick of Cardinal Virtues and Deadly Sins, and long for the society of plain men and women. Of the persons who read the first Canto, not one in ten reaches the end of the first book, and not one in a hundred perseveres to the end of the poem. Very few and very weary are those who are in at the death of the Blatant Beast." [1] Macaulay knew well enough that the Blatant Beast did not die in the poem as Spenser left it.

The newspaper writers are great sinners, and what with the frequent ignorance and haste of the authors and the carelessness of the printers a complete farrago of nonsense is sometimes concocted between them. A proper name is seldom given correctly in a daily paper, and it is a

[1] *Edinburgh Review*, vol. liv. (1831), p. 452.

frequently heard remark that no notice of
an event is published in which an error in
the names or qualifications of the actors
in it "is not detected by those acquainted
with the circumstances." The contributor
of the following bit of information to the
Week's News (Nov. 18th, 1871) must
have had a very vague notion of what a
monosyllable is, or he would not have
written, " The author of *Dorothy, De
Cressy*, etc., has another novel nearly
ready for the press, which, with the writer's
partiality for monosyllabic titles, is named
Thomasina." He is perhaps the same
person who remarked on the late Mr.
Robertson's fondness for monosyllables
as titlesfor his plays, and after instancing
Caste, Ours, and *School*, ended his list with
Society. We can, however, fly at higher
game than this, for some twenty years ago
a writer in the *Times* fell into the mistake
of describing the entrance of one of the
German states into the Zollverein in terms
that proved him to be labouring under
the misconception that the great Customs-
Union was a new organisation. Another
source of error in the papers is the hurry

with which bits of news are printed before they have been authenticated. Each
editor wishes to get the start of his neigh-
bour, and the consequence is that they
are frequently deceived. In a number of
the *Literary Gazette* for 1837 there is a
paragraph headed "Sir Michael Faraday,"
in which the great philosopher is con-
gratulated upon the title which had been
conferred upon him. Another source of
blundering is the attempt to answer an
opponent before his argument is thoroughly understood. A few years ago a
gentleman made a note in the *Notes and
Queries* to the effect that a certain custom
was at least 1400 years old, and was probably introduced into England in the fifth
century. Soon afterwards another gentleman wrote to the same journal, "Assuredly
this custom was general before A.D. 1400 ";
but how he obtained that date out of the
previous communication no one can tell.

The *Times* made a strange blunder in
describing a gallery of pictures : " Mr.
Robertson's group of ' Susannah and the
Elders,' with the name of Pordenone,
contains some passages of glowing colour

which must be set off against a good deal of clumsy drawing in the central figure of the chaste *maiden*." As bad as this was the confusion in the mind of the critic of the New Gallery, who spoke of Mr. Hallé's *Paolo and Francesca* as that masterly study and production of the old Adam phase of human nature which Milton hit off so sublimely in the *Inferno*.

A writer in the *Notes and Queries* confused Beersheba with Bathsheba, and conferred on the woman the name of the place.

It has often been remarked that a thorough knowledge of the English Bible is an education of itself, and a correspondence in the *Times* in August 1888 shows the value of a knowledge of the Liturgy of the Church of England. In a leading article occurred the passage, " We have no doubt whatever that Scotch judges and juries will administer indifferent justice " A correspondent in Glasgow, who supposed *indifferent* to mean *inferior*, wrote to complain at the insinuation that a Scotch jury would not do its duty. The editor of the *Times* had little

difficulty in answering this by referring to
the prayer for the Church militant, where
are the words, "Grant unto her [the
Queen's] whole Council and to all that
are put in authority under her, that they
may truly and indifferently minister justice,
to the punishment of wickedness and vice,
and to the maintenance of Thy true
religion, and virtue."

The compiler of an Anthology made
the following remarks in his preface : "In
making a selection of this kind one sails
between Scylla and Charybdis—the hack-
neyed and the strange. I have done my
best to steer clear of both these rocks."
A leader-writer in a morning paper a
few months ago made the same blunder
when he wrote : "As a matter of fact, Mr.
Gladstone was bound to bump against
either Scylla or Charybdis." It has generally been supposed that Scylla only was
a rock.

A most extraordinary blunder was made
in *Scientific American* eight or ten years
ago. An engraving of a handsome Chelsea china vase was presented with the
following description : " In England no

regular hard porcelain is made, but a
soft porcelain of great beauty is produced from kaolin, phosphate of lime,
and calcined silica.   The principal works
are situated at Chelsea.   The export of
these English porcelains is considerable,
and it is a curious fact that they are
largely imported into China, where they
are highly esteemed.   Our engraving
shows a richly ornamented vase in soft
porcelain from the works at Chelsea."
It could scarcely have been premised
that any one would be so ignorant as
to suppose that Chelsea china was still
manufactured, and this paragraph is a
good illustration of the evils of journalists
writing on subjects about which they know
nothing.

Critics who are supposed to be immaculate often blunder when sitting in judgment
on the sins of authors.   They are frequently puzzled by reprints, and led into
error by the disinclination of publishers
to give particulars in the preface as
to a book which was written many
years before its republication.   A few
years ago was issued a reprint of the

translation of the *Arabian Nights*, by Jonathan Scott, LL.D., which was first published in 1811. A reviewer having the book before him overlooked this important fact, and straightway proceeded to "slate" Dr. Scott for his supposed work of supererogation in making a new translation when Lane's held the field, the fact really being that Scott's translation preceded Lane's by nearly thirty years.

Another critic, having to review a re-print of Galt's *Lives of Players*, complained that Mr. Galt had not brought his book down to the date of publication, being ignorant of the fact that John Galt died as long ago as 1839. The reviewer of Lamb's *Tales from Shakespeare* committed the worst blunder of all when he wrote that those persons who did not know their Shakespeare might read Mr. Lamb's paraphrase if they liked, but for his part he did not see the use of such works. The man who had never heard of Charles Lamb and his *Tales* must have very much mistaken his vocation when he set up as a literary critic.

These are all genuine cases, but the

story of Lord Campbell and his criticism
of *Romeo and Juliet* is almost too good to
be true.   It is said that when the future
Lord Chancellor first came to London
he went to the editor of the *Morning
Chronicle* for some work.   The editor
sent him to the theatre.   " Plain John "
Campbell had no idea he was witnessing
a play of Shakespeare, and he therefore
set to work to sketch the plot of *Romeo
and Juliet,* and to give the author a little
wholesome advice.   He recommended a
curtailment in parts so as to render it
more suitable to the taste of a cultivated
audience.   We can quite understand that
if a story like this was once set into circulation it was not likely to be allowed to
die by the many who were glad to have a
laugh at the rising barrister.

CHAPTER III.

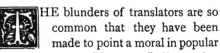HE blunders of translators are so common that they have been made to point a moral in popular proverbs. According to an Italian saying *translators are traitors* ("I traduttori sono traditori"); and books are said to be *done* into English, *traduced* in French, and *overset* in Dutch. Colton, the author of *Lacon*, mentions a half-starved German at Cambridge named Render, who had been long enough in England to forget German, but not long enough to learn English. This worthy, in spite of his deficiencies, was a voluminous translator of his native literature, and it became a proverbial saying among his intimates respecting a bad translation that it was *Rendered* into English.

The Comte de Tressan translated the

words " capo basso " (low headland) in a
passage from Ariosto by "Cap de Capo
Basso," on account of which translation
the wits insisted upon calling him " Comte
de Capo Basso."

Robert Hall mentions a comical stumble
made by one of the translators of Plato,
who construed through the Latin and not
direct from the Greek.   In the Latin
version *hirundo* stood as *hirŭdo*, and the
translator, overlooking the mark of con-
traction, declared to the astonished world
on the authority of Plato that the *horse-
leech* instead of the swallow was the har-
binger of spring.   Hoole, the translator of
Tasso and Ariosto, was as confused in his
natural history when he rendered " I
colubri Viscontei " or *Viscontian snakes*,
the crest of the Visconti family, as " the
Calabrian Viscounts."

As strange as this is the Frenchman's
notion of the presence of guns in the
canons' seats : " L'Archevêque de Can-
torbery avait fait placer des *canons* dans
les stalles de la cathédrale."   He quite
overlooked the word *chanoines*, which he
should have used.   This use of a word

similarly spelt is a constant source of trouble to the translator : for instance, a French translator of Scott's *Bride of Lammermuir* left the first word of the title untranslated, with the result that he made it the Bridle of Lammermuir, "La Bride de Lammermuir."

Thevenot in his travels refers to the fables of *Damné et Calilve*, meaning the *Hitopodesa*, or Pilpay's Fables. His translator calls them the fables of the damned Calilve. This is on a par with De Quincey's specimen of a French Abbé's Greek. Having to paraphrase the Greek words "'Ηροδοτος και ιαξων" (Herodotus even while Ionicizing), the Frenchman rendered them "Herodote et aussi Jazon," thus creating a new author, one Jazon. In the *Present State of Peru*, a compilation from the *Mercurio Peruano*, P. Geronymo Roman de la Higuera is transformed into "Father Geronymo, a Romance of La Higuera."

In Robertson's *History of Scotland* the following passage is quoted from Melville's *Account of John Knox* : " He was so active and vigorous a preacher that he was like

4

to ding the pulpit into blads and fly out
of it." M. Campenon, the translator of
Robertson into French, turns this into the
startling statement that he broke his pulpit
and leaped into the midst of his auditors.
A good companion to this curious "fact"
may be found in the extraordinary trope
used by a translator of Busbequius, who
says "his misfortunes had reduced him to
the top of all miseries."

We all know how Victor Hugo transformed the Frith of Forth into the First of
the Fourth, and then insisted that he was
right; but this great novelist was in the
habit of soaring far above the realm of
fact, and in a work he brought out as an
offering to the memory of Shakespeare he
showed that his imagination carried him
far away from historical facts. The author
complains in this book that the muse of
history cares more for the rulers than for
the ruled, and, telling only what is pleasant,
ignores the truth when it is unpalatable
to kings. After an outburst of bombast
he says that no history of England tells us
that Charles II. murdered his brother the
Duke of Gloucester. We should be sur-

prised if any did do so, as that young man died of small-pox. Hugo, being totally ignorant of English history, seems to have confused the son of Charles I. with an earlier Duke of Gloucester (Richard III.), and turned the assassin into the victim. After these blunders Dr. Baly's mention of the cannibals of *Nova Scotia* instead of *New Caledonia* in his translation of Müller's *Elements of Physiology* seems tame.

One snare that translators are constantly falling into is the use of English words which are like the foreign ones, but nevertheless are not equivalent terms, and translations that have taken their place in literature often suffer from this cause ; thus Cicero's *Offices* should have been translated *Duties*, and Marmontel never intended to write what we understand by *Moral Tales*, but rather tales of manners or of fashionable life. The translators of Calmet's *Dictionary of the Bible* render the French ancien, ancient, and write of "Mr. Huet, the ancient Bishop of Avranch." Theodore Parker, in translating a work by De Wette, makes the blunder of converting the German word *Wälsch*, a foreigner (in the book an equivalent for Italian), into *Welsh*.

Some men translate works in order to learn a language during the process, and they necessarily make blunders. It must have been one of these ignoramuses who translated *tellurische magnetismus* (terrestrial magnetism) as the magnetical qualities of Tellurium, and by his blunder caused an eminent chemist to test tellurium in order to find these magnetical qualities. There was more excuse for the French translator of one of Sir Walter Scott's novels who rendered a welsh rabbit (or rarebit, as it is sometimes spelt) into *un lapin du pays de Galles*. Walpole states that the Duchess of Bolton used to divert George I. by affecting to make blunders, and once when she had been to see Cibber's play of *Love's Last Shift* she called it *La dernière chemise de l'amour*. A like translation of Congreve's *Mourning Bride* is given in good faith in the first edition of Peignot's *Manuel du Bibliophile*, 1800, where it is described as *L'Épouse de Matin*; and the translation which Walpole attributes to the Duchess of Bolton the French say was made by a Frenchman named La Place.

The title of the old farce *Hit or Miss* was turned into *Frappé ou Mademoiselle,* and the *Independent Whig* into *La Perruque Indépendante.*

In a late number of the *Literary World* the editor, after alluding to the French translator of Sir Walter Scott who turned "a sticket minister" into "le ministre assassiné," gives from the *Bibliothèque Universelle* the extraordinary translation of the title of Mr. Barrie's comedy, *Walker, London,* as *Londres qui se promène.*

Old translators have played such tricks with proper names as to make them often unintelligible; thus we find La Rochefoucauld figuring as Ruchfucove; and in an old treatise on the mystery of Freemasonry by John Leland, Pythagoras is described as Peter Gower the Grecian. This of course is an Anglicisation of the French Pythagore (pronounced like Peter Gore). Our versions of Eastern names are so different from the originals that when the

two are placed together there appears
to be no likeness between them, and the
different positions which they take up in
the alphabet cause the bibliographer an
infinity of trouble. Thus the original of
Xerxes is Khshayarsha (the revered king),
and Averrhoes is Ibn Roshd (son of
Roshd). The latter's full name is Abul
Walid Mohammed ben Ahmed ben Mohammed. Artaxerxes is in old Persian
Artakhshatra, or the Fire Protector, and
Darius means the Possessor. Although
all these names—Xerxes, Artaxerxes, and
Darius—have a royal significance, they
were personal names, and not titles like
Pharaoh.

It is often difficult to believe that translators can have taken the trouble to read
their own work, or they surely would not
let pass some of the blunders we meet
with. In a translation of Lamartine's
Girondins some courtly people are described as figuring "under the vaults" of
the Tuileries instead of beneath the arched
galleries (*sous ses voutes*). This, however, is nothing to a blunder to be found
in the *Secret Memoirs of the Court of*

Louis XIV. and of the Regency (1824). The following passage from the original work, "Deux en sont morts et on dit publiquement qu'ils ont été empoisonnés," is rendered in the English translation to the confusion of common sense as " Two of them died with her, and said publicly that they had been poisoned."

This is not unlike the bull of the young soldier who, writing home in praise of the Indian climate, said, " But a lot of young fellows come out here, and they drink and they eat, and they eat and they drink, and they die ; and then they write home to their friends saying it was the climate that did it."

Some authors have found that there is peril in too free a translation, thus Dotet was condemned on Feb. 14th, 1543, for translating a passage in Plato's Dialogues as " After death you will be nothing *at all.*" Surely he who translated *Dieu défend l'adultère* as *God defends adultery* more justly deserved punishment ! Guthrie, the geographical writer, who translated a French book of travels, unfortunately mistook *neuvième* (ninth) for *nouvelle* or

neuve, and therefore made an allusion to
the twenty-sixth day of the new moon.

Moore quotes in his *Diary* (Dec.
30th, 1818) a most amusing blunder of
a translator who knew nothing of the
technical name for a breakwater. He
translated the line in Goldsmith's *Deserted
Village,*

> " As ocean sweeps the labour'd mole away,"

into

> "Comme la mer détruit les travaux de la
> taupe."

D'Israeli records two comical translations from English into French. " Ainsi
douleur, va-t'en " for *woe begone* is almost
too good ; and the man who mistook the
expression " the officer was broke " as
meaning broke on a wheel and translated
it by *roué* made a very serious matter of
what was possibly but a small fault.

In the translation of *The Conscript* by
Erckmann-Chatrian, the old botcher is
turned into the old butcher.

Sometimes in attempting to correct a
supposed blunder of another we fall into

a very real one of our own. Thus a few years ago, before we knew so much about folk-lore as we do now, we should very probably have pointed out that Cinderella's glass slipper owed its existence to a misprint. Fur was formerly so rare and so highly prized that its use was restricted by sumptuary laws to kings, princes, and persons holding honourable offices. In these laws sable is called vair, and it has been asserted that Perrault marked the dignity conferred upon Cinderella by the fairy's gift of a slipper of vair, a privilege confined to the highest rank of princesses. It is further stated that by an error of the printer *vair* was changed into *verre*. Now, however, we find in the various versions which have been collected of this favourite tale that, however much the incidents may differ, the slipper is almost invariably made of some rigid material, and in the earliest forms the unkind sisters cut their feet to make them fit the slipper. This unpleasant incident was omitted by Perrault, but he kept the rigid material and made the glass slipper famous.

The Revisers of the Old Testament

translation have shown us that the famous
verse in Job, " Oh that mine adversary
had written a book," is wrong; but it
will never drop out of our language
and literature. The Revised Version is
certainly much more in accordance with
our ideas of the time when the book was
written, a period when authors could not
have been very common :—

" Oh that I had one to hear me !
    (Lo, here is my signature, let the Almighty
        answer me ;)
    And that I had the indictment which mine
        adversary hath written !
    Surely I would carry it upon my shoulder ;
    I would bind it unto me as a crown."

Silk Buckingham drew attention to the
fact that some translations of the Bible
had been undertaken by persons ignorant
of the idioms of the language into which
they were translating, and he gave an
instance from an Arabic translation where
the text " Judge not, that ye be not
judged " was rendered " Be not just to
others, lest others should be just to
you."

The French have tried ingeniously to

explain the difficulty contained in *St. Matthew* xix. 24, " It is easier for a camel to go through the eye of a needle than for a rich man to enter into the kingdom of God," by affirming that the translators mistook the supposed word κάμιλος, a rope, for κάμηλος, a camel.

The humours of translation are numerous, but perhaps the most eccentric example is to be found in Stanyhurst's rendering of *Virgil*, published in 1583. It is full of cant words, and reads like the work of a madman. This is a fair specimen of the work :—

> " Theese thre were upbotching, not shapte, but
> partlye wel onward,
> A clapping fierbolt (such as oft, with rownce
> robel-hobble,
> Jove to the ground clattreth) but yeet not
> finished holye."

M. Guyot, translating some Latin epigrams under the title of *Fleurs, Morales, et Épigrammatiques,* uses the singular forms Monsieur Zoïle and Mademoiselle Lycoris. The same author, when translating the letters of Cicero (1666), turns Pomponius into M. de Pomponne.

Pitt's friend, Pepper Arden, Master of
the Rolls, Lord Chief Justice of the
Common Pleas and Lord Alvanley, was
rather hot-tempered, and his name was
considered somewhat appropriate, but to
make it still more so his friends translated
it into " Mons. Poivre Ardent."

This reminds one of the Frenchman who
toasted Dr. Johnson, not as Mr. Rambler,
but as Mr. Vagabond.

Tom Moore notices some amusing mis-
translations in his *Diary*. Major Cart-
wright, who was called the Father of
Reform (although a wit suggested that
Mother of Reform would have been a
more appropriate title), supposed that
the *Brevia Parliamentaria* of Prynne
stood for "short parliaments." Lord
Lansdowne told Moore that he was with
Lord Holland when the letter containing
this precious bit of erudition arrived.
Another story of Lord Lansdowne's is
equally good. His French servant announced Dr. Mansell, the Master of
Trinity, when he called, as " Maître des
Cérémonies de la Trinité."

Moore also relates that an account

having appeared in the London papers of a row at the Stock Exchange, where some strangers were hustled, it appeared in the Paris papers in this form: "Mons. Stock Exchange était échauffé," etc.

There is something to be said in favour of the humorous translation of *Magna est veritas et prevalabit*—"Great is truth, and it will prevail a bit," for it is probably truer than the original. He who construed Cæsar's mode of passing into Gaul *summa diligentia*, "on the top of the diligence," must have been of an imaginative turn of mind. Probably the time will soon come when this will need explanation, for a public will arise which knows not the dilatory "diligence."

The translator of *Inter Calicem supremaque labra* as Betwixt Dover and Calais gave as his reason that Dover was *Angliæ suprema labra*.

Although not a blunder nor apparently a joke, we may conclude this chapter with a reference to Shakespeare's remarkable translation of *Finis Coronat opus*. Helena remarks in *All's well that Ends well* (act iv., sc. 4) :—

" All's well that ends well : still *the fine's the crown.*"

In the *Second Part of King Henry VI.* (act v., sc. 2) old Lord Clifford, just before he dies, is made to use the French translation of the proverb :—

" La fin couronne les œuvres."

In the first Folio we read :—

" La fin corrone les eumenes."

CHAPTER IV.

BIBLIOGRAPHICAL BLUNDERS.

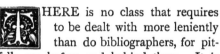 HERE is no class that requires to be dealt with more leniently than do bibliographers, for pit-falls are before and behind them. It is impossible for any one man to see all the books he describes in a general biblio-graphy ; and, in consequence of the neces-sity of trusting to second-hand information, he is often led imperceptibly into gross error. Watt's *Bibliotheca Britannica* is a most useful and valuable work, but, as may be expected from so comprehensive a compilation, many mistakes have crept into it: for instance, under the head of Philip Beroaldus, we find the following title of a work : " A short view of the Persian Monarchy, published at the end of Daniel's Works." The mystery of the last part of the title is cleared up when we

find that it should properly be read, " *and of Daniel's Weekes,*" it being a work on prophecy. The librarian of the old Marylebone Institution, knowing as little of Latin as the monk did of Hebrew when he described a book as having the beginning where the end should be, catalogued an edition of Æsop's Fables as " *Æsopiarum's Phœdri Fabulorum.*"

Two blunders that a bibliographer is very apt to fall into are the rolling of different authors of the same name into one, and the creation of an author who never existed. The first kind we may illustrate by mentioning the dismay of the worthy Bishop Jebb, when he found himself identified in Watt's *Bibliotheca* with his uncle, the Unitarian writer. Of the second kind we might point out the names of men whose lives have been written and yet who never existed. In the *Zoological Biography* of Agassiz, published by the Ray Society, there is an imaginary author, by name J. K. Broch, whose work, *Entomologische Briefe*, was published in 1823. This pamphlet is really anonymous, and was written by one who signed himself J. K. Broch. is merely an explanation in the catalogue from which the entry was taken that it was a *brochure.* Moreri created an author, whom he styled Dorus Basilicus, out of the title of James I.'s Δῶρον βασιλικὸν, and Bishop Walton supposed the title of the great Arabic Dictionary, the *Kamoos* or Ocean, to be the name of an author whom he quotes as " Camus." In the article on Stenography in Rees's Cyclopædia there are two most amusing blunders. John Nicolai published a *Treatise on the Signs of the Ancients* at the beginning of the last century, and the writer of the article, having seen it stated that a certain fact was to be found in Nicolai, jumped to the conclusion that it was the name of a place, and wrote, " It was at Nicolai that this method of writing was first introduced to the Greeks by Xenophon himself." In another part of the same article the oldest method of shorthand extant, entitled " Ars Scribendi Characteris," is said to have been printed about the year 1412—that is, long before printing was invented. In the *Biographie Univer-*

5

selle there is a life of one Nicholas Donis,
by Baron Walckenaer, which is a blundering alteration of the real name of a Bene-
dictine monk called Dominus Nicholas.
This, however, is not the only time that
a title has been taken for a name. An
eminent bookseller is said to have received a letter signed George Winton,
proposing a life of Pitt ; but, as he did not
know the name, he paid no attention to
the letter, and was much astonished when
he was afterwards told that his correspondent was no less a person than
George Pretyman Tomline, Bishop of
Winchester. This is akin to the mistake
of the Scotch doctor attending on the
Princess Charlotte during her illness, who
said that "ane Jean Saroom" had been
continually calling, but, not knowing the
fellow, he had taken no notice of him.
Thus the Bishop of Salisbury was sent
away by one totally ignorant of his dignity. A similar blunder was made by a
bibliographer, for in Hotten's *Handbook
to the Topography and Family History of
England and Wales* will be found an entry
of an "Assize Sermon by Bishop Wigorn,

in the Cathedral at Worcester, 1690." This was really Bishop Stillingfleet. There is a reverse case of a catalogue made by a worthy bookseller of the name of William London, which was long supposed to be the work of Dr. William Juxon, the Bishop of London at the time of publication. The entry in the *Biographie Moderne* of "Brigham *le jeune* ou Brigham Young" furnishes a fine instance of a writer succumbing to the ever-present temptation to be too clever by half. A somewhat similar blunder is that of the late Mr. Dircks. The first reprint of the Marquis of Worcester's *Century of Inventions* was issued by Thomas Payne, the highly respected bookseller of the Mews Gate, in 1746; but in *Worcesteriana* (1866) Mr. Dircks positively asserts that the notorious Tom Paine was the publisher of it, thus ignoring the different spelling of the two names.

In a French book on the invention of printing, the sentence "Le berceau de l'imprimerie" was misread by a German, who turned Le Berceau into a man D'Israeli tells us that *Mantissa*, the title of the Appendix to Johnstone's *History of Plants*, was taken for the name of an author by D'Aquin, the French king's physician. The author of the *Curiosities of Literature* also relates that an Italian misread the description *Enrichi de deux listes* on the title-page of a French book of travels, and, taking it for the author's name, alluded to the opinions of Mons. Enrichi De Deux Listes; but really this seems almost too good to be true.

If we searched bibliographical literature we should find a fair crop of authors who never existed; for when once a blunder of this kind is set going, it seems to bear a charmed life. Mr. Daydon Jackson mentions some amusing instances of imaginary authors made out of title-pages in his *Guide to the Literature of Botany*. An anonymous work of A. Massalongo, entitled *Graduale Passagio delle Crittogame alle Fanerogame* (1876), has been entered in a German bibliography as written by G. Passagio. In an English list Kelaart's *Flora Calpensis: Reminiscences of Gibraltar* (1846) appears as the work of a lady—

Christian name, Flora; *surname,* Calpensis.
In 1837 a *Botanical Lexicon* was published
by an author who described himself as
"The Rev. Patrick Keith, Clerk, F.L.S."
This somewhat pedantic form deceived a
foreign cataloguer, who took Clerk for the
surname, and contracted "Patrick Keith"
into the initials P.K. More inexcusable
was the blunder of an American who, in
describing J. E. H. Gordon's work on
Electricity, changed the author's degree
into the initials of a collaborator, one
Cantab. The joint authors were stated
to be J. E. H. Gordon and B. A. Cantab.

A very amusing, but a quite excusable
error, was made by Allibone in his
Dictionary of English Literature, under
the heading of Isaac D'Israeli. He
notices new editions of that author's
works revised by the Right Hon. the
Chancellor of the Exchequer, of course
Isaac's son Benjamin, afterwards Prime
Minister and Earl of Beaconsfield; but
unfortunately there were two Chancellors
in 1858, and Allibone chooses the wrong
one, printing, as useful information to the
reader, that the reviser was Sir George

Cornewall Lewis. An instance of the danger of inconsiderate explanation will be found in a little book by a German lady, Fanny Lewald, entitled *England and Schottland.* The authoress, when in London, visited the theatre in order to see a play founded on Cooper's novel *The Wept of Wish-ton Wish*; and being unable to understand the title, she calls it the " Will of the Whiston Wisp," which she tells us means an *ignis fatuus.*

A writer in a German paper was led into an amusing blunder by an English review a few years ago. The reviewer, having occasion to draw a distinction between George and Robert Cruikshank, spoke of the former as the real Simon Pure. The German, not understanding the allusion, gravely told his readers that George Cruikshank was a pseudonym, the author's real name being Simon Pure. This seems almost too good to be equalled, but a countryman of our own has blundered nearly as grossly. William Taylor, in his *Historic Survey of German Poetry* (1830), prints the following absurd statement: " Godfred of Berlichingen is one of the earliest imitations of the Shakspeare tragedy which the German school has produced. It was admirably translated into English in 1799 at Edinburg by *William* Scott, advocate, no doubt the same person who, under the poetical but assumed name of *Walter*, has since become the most extensively popular of the British writers." The cause of this mistake we cannot explain, but the reason for it is to be found in the fact which has lately been announced that a few copies of the translation, with the misprint of William for Walter in the title, were issued before the error was discovered.

Jacob Boehm, the theosophist, wrote some Reflections on a theological treatise by one Isaiah Stiefel,[1] the title of which puzzled one of his modern French biographers. The word Stiefel in German means a boot, and the Frenchman therefore gave the title of Boehm's tract as " Reflexions sur les Bottes d'Isaie."

It is scarcely fair to make capital out

---

[1] "*Bedencken über Esaiæ Stiefels Buchlein: von dreyerley Zustandt des Menschen unnd dessen newen Geburt.*" 1639.

of the blunders of booksellers' catalogues, which are often printed in a great hurry, and cannot possibly possess the advantage of correction which a book does.   But one or two examples may be given without any censure being intended on the booksellers.

In a French catalogue the works of the famous philosopher Robert Boyle appeared under the following singular French form : BOY (le), Chymista scepticus vel dubia et paradoxa chymico-physica, &c.

"Mr. Tul. Cicero's Epistles" looks strange, but the mistake is but small. The very natural blunder respecting the title of Shelley's *Prometheus Unbound* actually did occur ; and, what is more, it was expected by Theodore Hook.   This is an accurate copy of the description in the catalogue of a year or two back :—

"Shelley's Prometheus *Unbound.*

——— another copy, *in whole calf.*"

and these are Hook's lines :—

"Shelley styles his new poem 'Prometheus Un-
    bound,'
And 'tis like to remain so while time circles
    round ;

For surely an age would be spent in the finding
A reader so weak as *to pay for the binding.*"

When books are classified in a catalogue
the compiler must be peculiarly on his
guard if he has the titles only and not
the books before him. Sometimes instances of incorrect classification show
gross ignorance, as in the instance quoted
in the *Athenæum* lately. Here we have
a crop of blunders : " *Title,* Commentarii
De Bello Gallico in usum Scholarum
Liber Tirbius. *Author,* Mr. C. J.
Caesoris. *Subject,* Religion." Still better
is the auctioneer's entry of P. V. Maroni's
The Opera. Authors, however, are usually
so fond of fanciful ear-catching titles, that
every excuse must be made for the cataloguer, who mistakes their meaning, and
takes them in their literal signification.
Who can reprove too severely the classi-
fier who placed Swinburne's *Under the
Microscope* in his class of *Optical Instruments,* or treated Ruskin's *Notes on the
Construction of Sheepfolds* as a work on
agricultural appliances ? A late instance
of an amusing misclassification is reported
from Germany. In the *Orientalische*

Bibliographie, Mr. Rider Haggard's wonderful story *King Solomon's Mines* is entered as a contribution to "Alttestamentliche Litteratur."

The elaborate work by Careme, *Le Patissier Pittoresque* (1842), which contains designs for confectioners, deceived the bookseller from its plates of pavilions, temples, etc., into supposing it to be a book on architecture, and he accordingly placed it under that heading in his catalogue.

Mr. Daydon Jackson gives several instances of false classification in his *Guide to the Literature of Botany*, and remarks that some authors contrive titles seemingly of set purpose to entrap the unwary. He instances a fine example in the case of Bishop Alexander Ewing's *Feamainn Earraghaidhiell : Argyllshire Seaweeds* (Glasgow, 1872. 8vo). To enhance the delusion, the coloured wrapper is ornamented with some of the common marine algæ, but the inside of the volume consists solely of pastoral addresses. Another example will be found in *Flowers from the South, from the Hortus Siccus of an*

Old Collector. By W. H. Hyett, F.R.S. Instead of a popular work on the Mediterranean flora by a scientific man, as might reasonably be expected, this is a volume of translations from the Italian and Latin poets. It is scarcely fair to blame the compiler of the *Bibliotheca Historico - Naturalis* for having ranked both these works among scientific treatises. The English cataloguer who treated as a botanical book Dr. Garnett's selection from Coventry Patmore's poems, entitled *Florilegium Amantis,* could claim less excuse for his blunder than the German had. These misleading titles are no new invention, and the great bibliographer Haller was deceived into including the title of James Howell's *Deudrologia, or Dodona's Grove* (1640), in his *Bibliotheca Botanica.* Professor Otis H. Robinson contributed a very interesting paper on the "Titles of Books" to the *Special Report on Public Libraries in the United States of America* (1876), in which he deals very fully with this difficulty of misleading titles, and some of his preliminary remarks are very much to the point. He writes :—

" No act of a man's life requires
more practical common sense than the
naming of his book. If he would make
a grocer's sign or an invoice of a cellar
of goods or a city directory, he uses no
metaphors ; his pen does not hesitate for
the plainest word. He must make himself understood by common men. But
if he makes a book the case is different.
It must have the charm of a pleasing
title. If there is nothing new within, the
back at least must be novel and taking.
He tortures his imagination for something
which will predispose the reader in its
favour. Mr. Parker writes a series of
biographical sketches, and calls it *Morning
Stars of the New World.* Somebody pre-
pares seven religious essays, binds them
up in a book, and calls it *Seven Stormy
Sundays.* Mr. H. T. Tuckerman makes
a book of essays on various subjects, and
calls it *The Optimist* ; and then devotes
several pages of preface to an argument,
lexicon in hand, proving that the applica-
bility of the term optimist is ' obvious.'
An editor, at intervals of leisure, indulges
his true poetic taste for the pleasure of his

friends, or the entertainment of an occa
sional audience. Then his book appears,
entitled not *Miscellaneous Poems,* but
Asleep in the Sanctum, by A. A. Hopkins.
Sometimes, not satisfied with one enigma,
another is added. Here we have *The
Great Iron Wheel ; or, Republicanism Back-
wards and Christianity Reversed,* by J. R.
Graves. These titles are neither new nor
scarce, nor limited to any particular class
of books. Every case, almost every shelf,
in every library contain such. They are as
old as the art of book-making. David's
lamentation over Saul and Jonathan was
called *The Bow.* A single word in the
poem probably suggested the name. Three
of the orations of Æschines were styled *The
Graces,* and his letters *The Muses.*"

The list of bibliographical blunders
might be indefinitely extended, but the
subject is somewhat technical, and the
above few instances will give a sufficient
indication of the pitfalls which lie in the
way of the bibliographer—a worker who
needs universal knowledge if he is to
wend his way safely through the snares
in his path.

CHAPTER V.

LISTS OF ERRATA.

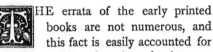HE errata of the early printed books are not numerous, and this fact is easily accounted for when we recollect that these books were superintended in their passage through the press by scholars such as the Alduses, Andreas, Bishop of Aleria, Campanus Perottus, the Stephenses, and others. It is said that the first book with a printed errata is the edition of *Juvenal*, with notes of Merula, printed by Gabriel Pierre, at Venice, in 1478 ; previously the mistakes had been corrected by the pen. One of the longest lists of errata on record, which occupies fifteen folio pages, is in the edition of the works of Picus of Mirandula, printed by Knoblauch, at Strasburg, in 1507. A worse case of blundering will be found in a little book of only one

hundred and seventy-two pages, entitled *Missæ ac Missalis Anatomia*, 1561, which contains fifteen pages of errata. The author, feeling that such a gross case of blundering required some excuse or explanation, accounted for the misprints by asserting that the devil drenched the manuscript in the kennel, making it almost illegible, and then obliged the printer to misread it. We may be allowed to believe that the fiend who did all the mischief was the printer's "devil."

Cardinal Bellarmin tried hard to get his works printed correctly, but without success, and in 1608 he was forced to publish at Ingolstadt a volume entitled *Recognitio librorum omnium Roberti Bellarmini*, in which he printed eighty-eight pages of errata of his Controversies.

Edward Leigh, in his thin folio volume entitled *On Religion and Learning*, 1656, was forced to add two closely printed leaves of errata.

Sometimes apparent blunders have been intentionally made ; thus, to escape the decree of the Inquisition that the words fatum and fata should not be used in

any work, a certain author printed *facta*
in his book, and added in the errata "*for*
facta *read* fata."

In dealing with our own older literature
we find a considerable difference in degree
of typographical correctness ; thus the old
plays of the sixteenth and seventeenth
centuries are often marvels of inaccuracy,
and while books of the same date are
usually supplied with tables of errata,
plays were issued without any such helps
to correction.   This to some extent is to
be accounted for by the fact that many of
these plays were surreptitious publications,
or, at all events, printed in a hurry, without
care. The late Mr. Halliwell Phillipps, in
his curious privately printed volume (*A
Dictionary of Misprints*, 1887), writes :
"Such tests were really a thousandfold
more necessary in editions of plays, but
they are practically non-existent in the
latter, the brief one which is prefixed
to Dekker's *Satiro-Mastix*, 1602, being
nearly the only example that is to be
found in any that appeared during the
literary career of the great dramatist."

In other branches of literature it is

evident that some care was taken to escape misprints, either by the correction of the printer's reader or of the author. Some of the excuses made for misprints in our old books are very amusing. In a little English book of twenty-six leaves printed at Douay in 1582, and entitled *A true reporte of the death and martyrdome of M. Campion Jesuite and Preiste, and M. Sherwin and M. Bryan Preistes, at Tiborne the first of December* 1581, is this notice at the end :—

"Good reader, pardon all faultes escaped in the printing and beare with the woorkmanship of a strainger."

Many of Nicholas Breton's tracts were issued surreptitiously, and he protested that many pieces which he had never written were falsely ascribed to him. *The Bower of Delights* was published without the author's sanction, and the printer (or publisher) Richard Jones made the following address "to the Gentlemen Readers" on the blunders which had been made in the book :—

"Pardon mee (good Gentlemen) of my presumption, & protect me, I pray you,

6

against those Cavellers and findfaults, that
never like of any thing that they see
printed, though it be never so well compiled. And where you happen to find
fault, impute it to bee committed by the
Printers negligence, then (otherwise) by
any ignorance in the author : and especially in A 3, about the middest of
the page, for LIME OR LEAD I pray you
read LINE OR LEAD. So shall your poore
Printer haue just cause hereafter to be
more carefull, and acknowledge himselfe
most bounden (at all times) to do your
service to the utmost of his power.

"Yours R. J., PRINTER."

A little scientific book, entitled *The
Making and use of the Geometricall Instrument called a Sector . . . by Thomas Hood*,
1598, has a list of errata headed *Faultes
escaped*, with this note of the author
or printer :—

"Gentle reader, I pray you excuse
these faults, because I finde by ex-
perience, that it is an harder matter to
print these mathematicall books trew,
then bookes of other discourse."

Arthur Hopton's *Baculum Geodæticum sive Viaticum or the Geodeticall Staffe* (1610), contains the following quaint lines at the head of the list of errata :—

"The Printer to the Reader.
" For errours past or faults that scaped be,
Let this collection give content to thee :
A worke of art, the grounds to us unknowne,
May cause us erre, thoughe all our skill be
showne.
When points and letters, doe containe the sence,
The wise may halt, yet doe no great offence.
Then pardon here, such faults that do befall,
The next edition makes amends for all."

Thomas Heywood, the voluminous dramatist, added to his *Apology for Actors* (1612) an interesting address to the printer of his tract, which, besides drawing attention to the printer's dislike of his errors being called attention to in a table of errata, is singularly valuable for its reference to Shakespeare's annoyance at Jaggard's treatment of him by attributing to his pen Heywood's poems from *Great Britain's Troy*.

"To my approved good Friend,
" MR. NICHOLAS OKES.
"The infinite faults escaped in my

booke of *Britaines Troy* by the negligence
of the printer, as the misquotations, mis-
taking the sillables, misplacing halfe lines,
coining of strange and never heard of
words, these being without number, when
I would have taken a particular account
of the *errata*, the printer answered me, hee
would not publish his owne disworkeman-
ship, but rather let his owne fault lye
upon the necke of the author. And being
fearefull that others of his quality had
beene of the same nature and condition,
and finding you, on the contrary, so
carefull and industrious, so serious and
laborious to doe the author all the rights
of the presse, I could not choose but
gratulate your honest indeavours with
this short remembrance. Here, likewise,
I must necessarily insert a manifest injury
done me in that worke, by taking the
two epistles of Paris to Helen, and Helen
to Paris, and printing them in a lesse
volume under the name of another, which
may put the world in opinion I might
steale them from him, and hee, to doe
himselfe right, hath since published them
in his owne name; but as I must ac-

knowledge my lines not worthy his patronage under whom he hath publisht them, so the author, I know, much offended with M. Jaggard (that altogether unknowne to him) presumed to make so bold with his name. These and the like dishonesties I knowe you to bee cleere of ; and I could wish but to bee the happy author of so worthy a worke as I could willingly commit to your care and workmanship.

"Yours ever, THOMAS HEYWOOD."

In the eighteenth century printers and authors had become hardened in their sins, and seldom made excuses for the errors of the press, but in the seventeenth century explanations were frequent.

Silvanus Morgan, in his *Horologiographia Optica. Dialling Universall and Particular, Speculative and Practicall, London* 1652, comes before his readers with these remarks on the errata :—

"Reader I having writ this some years since, while I was a childe in Art, and by this appear to be little more, for want of a review hath these faults, which I desire thee to mend with thy pen, and if there be any errour in art, as in chap. 17 which is only true at the time of the Equinoctiall, take that for an oversight, and where thou findest equilibra read equilibrio, and in the dedication (in some copies) read Robert Bateman for Thomas, and side for signe and know that *Optima prima cadunt, pessimus æve manent.*"

The list of errata in Joseph Glanvill's *Essays on several important subjects in Philosophy and Religion* (1676) is prefixed by this note :—

"The Reader is desired to take notice of the following Errours of the Press, some of which are so near in sound, to the words of the author, that they may easily be mistaken for his."

The next two books to be mentioned were published in the same year—1679. The noble author referred to in the first is that Roger Palmer who had the dishonour of being the husband of Charles II.'s notorious mistress, the Countess of Castle-maine.   Fortunately for the Earl she no longer bore his name, as she was created Duchess of Cleveland in 1670.   Professor De Morgan was inclined to doubt Lord

Castlemaine's authorship, but the following remarks by Joseph Moxon seem to prove that the peer did produce a rough draft of some kind :—

" Postscript concerning the Erratas and the Geographical part of this Globe," prefixed to *The English Globe* . . . by the Earl of Castlemaine :—

" The Erratas of the Press being many, I shall not set them down in a distinct Catalogue as usually, least the sight of them should more displease, than the particulars advantage, especially since they are not so material or intricate, but that any man may (I hope) easily mend them in the reading. I confess I have bin in a manner the occasion of them, by taking from the noble author a very foul copy, when he desir'd me to stay till a fair one were written over, so that truly 'tis no wonder, if workmen should in these cases not only sometimes leave out, but adde also, by taking one line for another, or not observing with exactness what words have bin wholly obliterated or dasht out."

John Playford, the music publisher and author, makes some remarks on the

subject of misprints in the preface to
his *Vade Mecum, or the Necessary Companion* (1679), which are worth quotation
here :—

" My profession obliging me to be
conversant with mathematical Books (the
printing whereof and musick, has been
my chiefest employment), I have observ'd
two things many times the cause why
Books of this nature appear abroad not
so correct as they should be ; either 1
Because they are too much hastened from
the Press, and not time enough allowed
for the strict and deliberate examination
of them ; which in all books ought to be
done, especially in these, for as much as
one false figure in a Mathematical book,
may prove a greater fault than a whole
word mistake in books of another kind.
Or, 2 Because Persons take Tables upon
trust without trying them, and with them
transcribe their errors, if not increase
them. Both these I have carefully avoided,
so that I have reason to believe (and think
I may say it without vanity) there never
was Tables more exactly printed than in
this Book, especially those for money and

annuities, for not trusting to my first calculation of them, I new calculated every
Table when it was in print, by the first
printed sheet, and when I had so done
I strictly compared it with my first calculation."

De Morgan registers the nineteenth
edition of this book, dated 1756, in his
Arithmetical Books, and he did not apparently know that it was originally published
so early as 1679.

In Morton's *Natural History of North-
amptonshire* (1712), is a list headed "Some
Errata of the press to be corrected"; and
at the end of the list is the following
amusing note: "There is no cut of the
Hen of the lesser Py'd Brambling in Tab.
13 tho' 'tis referred to in p. 423 which
omission was owing to an accident and is
really not very material, the hen of that
bird differing but little from the cock
which is represented in that Table under
fig. 3."

There is a very prevalent notion that
authors did not correct the proofs of their
books in the sixteenth and seventeenth
centuries, but there is sufficient evidence

that this is altogether a mistake. Professor
De Morgan, with his usual sagacity, alludes
to this point in his *Arithmetical Books*
(1847): " A great many circumstances in-
duce me to think that the general fashion
of correcting the press by the author came
in with the seventeenth century or there-
abouts." And he instances this note on
the title-page of Richard Witt's *Arithmetical Questions* (1613): "Examined also
and corrected at the Presse by the author
himselfe."

The late Dr. Brinsley Nicholson raised
this question in *Notes and Queries* in 1889,
and by his research it is possible to ante-
date the practice by nearly forty years.
For several of the following quotations I
am indebted to that invaluable periodical.
In Scot's *Hop-Garden* (1574) we find the
following excuse :—

" Forasmuch as M. Scot could not
be present at the printing of this his
booke, whereby I might have used his
advice in the correction of the same, and
especiallie of the Figures and Portrat-
ures conteyned therein, whereof he
delivered unto me such notes as I

being unskilfull in the matter could not so thoroughly conceyve, nor so perfectly expresse as . . . the authour or you."

In *The Droomme of Doomes Day.* By George Gascoigne (1576) is :—

" An Aduertisement of the Prynter to the Reader.

"Understand (gentle Reader) that whiles this worke was in the presse it pleased God to visit the translatour thereof with sicknesse. So that being unable himselfe to attend the dayly proofes, he apoynted a seruaunt of his to ouersee the same. Who being not so well acquainted with the matter as his maister was, there haue passed some faultes much contrary unto both our meanings and desires. The which I have therefore collected into this Table. Desiring every Reader that wyll vouchsafe to peruse this booke, that he will firste correct those faultes and then judge accordingly."

A particularly interesting note on this point precedes the list of errata in Stanyhurst's Translation of Virgil's *Æneid* (1582),

which was printed at Leyden. Mr. F. C.
Birkbeck Terry, who pointed this out in
Notes and Queries, quoted from Arber's
reprint, p. 157 :—

"John Pates Printer to thee Corteous
Reader, I am too craue thy pacience and
paynes (good reader) in bearing wyth such
faultes as haue escapte in printing: and
in correcting as wel such as are layd downe
heere too thy view, as all oother whereat
thou shalt hap too stumble in perusing
this treatise. Thee nooueltye of imprinting
English in theese partes and thee absence
of the author from perusing soome proofes
could not choose but breede errours."

Certainly Scot, Gascoigne, and Stanyhurst did not correct the proofs, but it
would not have been necessary to make
an excuse if the practice was not a pretty
general one among authors.

Bishop Babington's *Exposition of the
Lord's Prayer* (1588) contains an excuse
for the author's inability to correct the
press :—

" If thou findest any other faultes either
in words or distinctions troubling a perfect
sence (Gentle Reader) helpe them by thine

owne judgement and excuse the presse by the Authors absence, who best was acquainted to reade his owne hande."

In the Bodleian Library is preserved the printer's copy of Book V. of Hooker's *Ecclesiastical Polity* (1597), with Whitgift's signature and corrections in Hooker's handwriting. On one of the pages is the following note by the printer :—

" Good Mr. Hooker, I pray you be so good as to send us the next leaf that followeth this, for I know not by what mischance this of ours is lost, which standeth uppon the finishing of the book." [1]

Another proof of the general practice will be found in N. Breton's *The Wit of Wit* (1599) :—

" What faultes are escaped in the printing, finde by discretion, and excuse the Author by other worke that let him from attendance to the Presse ; non hà che non sà.   N. B. Gent."

At the end of Nash's dedication " To his Readers," *Lenten Stuffe* (1599), is this

---

[1] *Notes and Queries*, 7th Series, viii. 73.

interesting statement : " Apply it for me
for I am called away to correct the faults
of the press, that escaped in my absence
from the printing house."

Richard Brathwaite, when publishing
his *Strappado for the Divell* (1615), made
an excuse for not having seen all the
proofs. The whole note is well worthy
of reproduction :—

" *Upon the Errata.*

" Gentlemen (*humanum est errare*), to
confirme which position, this my booke
(as many other are) hath his share of
errors ; so as I run *ad prælum tanquam
ad prælium, in typos quasi in scippos* ; but
my comfort is if I be strappadoed by the
multiplicite of my errors, it is but answer-
able to my title : so as I may seem to
diuine by my style, what I was to indure
by the presse.   Yet know judicious disposed gentlemen, that the intricacie of the
copie, and the absence of the author from
many important proofes were occasion of
these errors, which defects (if they bee
supplied by your generous convenience
and curtuous disposition) I doe vowe to

satisfie your affectionate care with a
more serious surueigh in my next impression. . . . For other errors as the
misplacing of commaes, colons, and
periods (which as they are in euerie
page obvious, so many times they invert
the sence), I referre to your discretion
(judicious gentle-men) whose lenity may
sooner supply them, then all my industry
can portray them."

In *The Mastive, or Young Whelpe of
the Olde Dogge, Epigrams and Satyres*
(1615), an anonymous work of Henry
Peacham, we read :—

" The faultes escaped in the Printing
(or any other omission) are to be excused
by reason of the authors absence from the
Presse, who thereto should have given
more due instructions."

Dr. Brinsley Nicholson urought forward
two very interesting passages on the correcting of proofs from old plays. The
first, which looks very like an allusion to
the custom, is from the 1601 edition of
Ben Jonson's *Every Man in his Humour*
(act. ii., sc. 3), where Lorenzo, junior,
says, " My father had the proving of your

copy, some houre before I saw it." The
second is from Fletcher's *The Nice Valour*
(1624 or 1625), act. iv., sc. 1. Lapet
says to his servant (the clown Goloshio),
"So bring me the last proof, this is
corrected"; and Goloshio having gone
and returned, the following ensues :—

> *Lap.*   What says my Printer now ?
> *Clown.* Here's your last Proof, Sir.
>   You shall have perfect Books now in a
>   twinkling.[1]

The following address, which contains
a curious excuse of Dr. Daniel Featley for
not having corrected the proofs of his
book *The Romish Fisher Caught in his own
Net* (1624), is very much to the point :—
    " I entreat the courteous reader to
understand that the greater part of the
book was printed in the time of the great
frost ; when by reason that the Thames
was shut up, I could not conveniently
procure the proofs to be brought unto
mee, before they were wrought off ; where-
upon it fell out that many very grosse
escapes passed the press, and (which was

----

[1] *Notes and Queries*, 7th Series, viii. 253.

the worst fault of all) the third part is left unpaged."

As a later example we may cite from Sir Peter Leycester's *Historical Antiquities* (1673), where we find this note : " Reader, By reason of the author's absence, several faults have escaped the press : those which are the most material thou art desir'd to amend, and to pardon them all."

Printed mistakes are usually considered by the sufferers matters of somewhat serious importance ; and we picture to ourselves an author stalking up and down his room and tearing his hair when he first discovers them ; but Benserade, the French poet, was able to make a joke of the subject. This is the *rondeau* which he placed at the end of his version of *Les Métamorphoses d'Ovide* :—

> " Pour moi, parmi des fautes innombrables,
> Je n'en connais que deux considérables,
> Et dont je fais ma déclaration,
> C'est l'entreprise et l'exécution ;
> A mon avis fautes irréparables
> Dans ce volume."

According to the *Scaligerana*, Cardan's treatise *De Subtilitate*, printed by Vascosan

in 1557, does not contain a single misprint; but, on the whole, it may be very
seriously doubted whether an immaculate
edition of any work ever issued from the
press. The story is well known of the
serious attempt made by the celebrated
Glasgow printers Foulis to free their edition
of *Horace* from any chance of error. They
caused the proof-sheets after revision to
be hung up at the gate of the University,
with the offer of a reward to any one who
discovered a misprint. In spite of all this
care there are, according to Dibdin, six
uncorrected errors in this edition.

According to Isaac Disraeli, the goal
of freedom from blunders was nearly
reached by Dom Joze Souza, with the
assistance of Didot in 1817, when he
published his magnificent edition of *As
Lusiadas* of Camoens. However, an uncorrected error was discovered in some
copies, occasioned by the misplacing of
one of the letters in the word *Lusitano*.
A like case occurred a few years ago at an
eminent London printer's. A certain book
was about to be printed, and instructions
were issued that special care was to be

taken with the printing. It was read over by the chief reader, and all seemed to have gone well, when a mistake was discovered upon the title-page.

It may be mentioned here, with respect to tables of errata, that they are frequently neglected in subsequent books. There are many books in which the same blunders have been repeated in various editions, although they had been pointed out in an early issue.

CHAPTER VI.

Misprints.

OF all literary blunders misprints are the most numerous, and no one who is conversant with the inside of a printing-office will be surprised at this ; in fact, he is more likely to be struck with the freedom from error of the innumerable productions issued from the press than to be surprised at the blunders which he may come across. The possibilities of error are endless, and a frequent cause is to be found in the final correction, when a line may easily get transposed. On this account many authors will prefer to leave a trivial error, such as a wrong stop, in a final revise rather than risk the possibilities of blundering caused by the unlocking of the type. Of course a large number of misprints are far from amusing, while a sense of fun will sometimes be obtained by a trifling transposition of letters. Authors must be on the alert for misprints, although ordinary misspellings should not be left for them by the printer's reader; but they are usually too intent on the structure of their own sentences to notice these misprints. The curious point is that a misprint which has passed through proof and revise unnoticed by reader and author will often be detected immediately the perfected book is placed in the author's hands. The blunder which has hitherto remained hidden appears to start out from the page, to the author's great disgust. One reason why misprints are overlooked is that every word is a sort of pictorial object to the eye. We do not spell the word, but we guess what it is by the first and last letters and its length, so that a wrong letter in the body of the word is easily overlooked.

It is an important help to the editor of a corrupt text to know what misprints are the most probable, and for this purpose the late Mr. Halliwell Phillipps printed for private circulation *A Dictionary of Misprints, found in printed books of the sixteenth and seventeenth centuries, compiled for the use of verbal critics and especially for those who are engaged in editing the works of Shakespeare and our other early Dramatists* (1887). In the note at the end of this book Mr. Phillipps writes: " The readiest access to those evidences will be found in the old errata, and it will be seen, on an examination of the latter, that misprints are abundant in final and initial letters, in omissions, in numerals, and in verbal transpositions; but unquestionably the most frequent in pronouns, articles, conjunctions, and prepositions. When we come to words outside the four latter, there is a large proportion of examples that are either of rare occurrence or unique. Some of the blunders that are recorded are sufficiently grotesque: *e.g., Ile starte thence poore* for *Ile starve their poore,—he formaketh what* for *the fire maketh hot.* It must, indeed, be confessed that the conjectural emendator, if he dispenses with the quasi-authority of contemporary precedents, has an all but unlimited range for the exercise of his ingenuity, the unsettled spellings of our ancestors rendering almost any emendation, however extravagant, a typographical possibility.   A large number of their misprints could only have been perpetrated in the midst of the old orthographies. Under no other conditions could *ice* have been converted into *ye*, *air* into *time*, *home* into *honey*, *attain* into *at any*, *sun* into *sinner*, *stone* into *story*, *deem* into *deny*, *dire* into *dry*, the old spellings of the italicised words being respectively, yce, yee, ayre, tyme, home, honie, attaine, att anie, sunne, sinner, stone, storie, deeme, denie, dire, drie.   The form of the long *s* should also be sometimes taken into consideration, for it could only have been owing to its use that such a word as *some* could have been misprinted *four*, *niece* for *wife*, *prefer* for *preserve*, *find* for *fifth*, the variant old spellings being foure, neese, preferre."

Among the instances of misprints given in this Dictionary may be noticed the following : actions *for* axioms, agreement *for* argument, all-eyes *for* allies, aloud *for* allowed, banish'd *for* ravish'd, cancel *for* cantel, candle *for* caudle, cursedness *for* ourselves, eye-sores *for* oysters, felicity *for* facility, Hector *for* nectar, intending *for* indenting, John for Jehu, Judges *for* Indies, scene *for* seene, sixteen *for* sexton, and *for* sixty-one, tops *for* toy, Venus *for* Venice.

In connection with this work may be mentioned the late Mr. W. Blades's *Shakspere and Typography, being an attempt to show Shakspere's personal connection with, and technical knowledge of the Art of Printing, also Remarks upon some common typographical errors with especial reference to the text of Shakspere* (1872), a small work of very great interest and value. Mr. Blades writes : "Now these typographical blunders will, in the majority of cases, be found to fall into one of three classes, viz. :—

"Errors of the ear ;

"Errors of the eye ; and

"Errors from what, in printers' language, is called 'a foul case.'

"I. *Errors of the Ear.*—Every compositor when at work reads over a few words of his copy, and retains them in his mind until his fingers have picked up the various types belonging to them. While the memory is thus repeating to itself a phrase, it is by no means unnatural, nor in practice is it uncommon, for some word or words to become unwittingly supplanted in the mind by others which are similar in sound. It was simply a mental transposition of syllables that made the actor exclaim,—

'My Lord, stand back and let the parson cough'

instead of

'My Lord, stand back and let the coffin pass.'
Richard III., i. 2.

And, by a slight confusion of sound, the word *mistake* might appear in type as *must take* :—

'So you mistake your husbands.'
Hamlet, iii. 2.

Again, *idle votarist* would easily become *idol votarist*—

'I am no idle votarist.'—*Timon,* iv. 3 ;

and *long delays* become transformed to *longer days*—

'This done, see that you take no long delays.'
Titus, iv. 2.

From the time of Gutenberg until now this similarity of sound has been a fruitful source of error among printers.

"II. *Errors of the Eye.*—The eye often misleads the hand of the compositor, especially if he be at work upon a crabbed manuscript or worn-out reprint.   Take out a dot, and *This time goes manly* becomes

> 'This tune goes manly.'—*Macbeth*, iv. 3.

So a clogged letter turns *What beast was't then ?* into *What boast was't then ?*—

> ' *Lady M.*   What beast was't then,
> That made you break this enterprise to
>   me ? '
>
> > *Macbeth*, i. 7.

Examples might be indefinitely multiplied from many an old book, so I will quote but one more instance.   The word *pre-serve* spelt with a long *s* might without much carelessness be misread *preferre* (1 *Henry VI.*, iii. 2), and thus entirely alter the sense.

"III. *Errors from a 'foul case.'*—This class of errors is of an entirely different

kind from the two former. They came
from within the man, and were from the
brain ; this is from without, mechanical in
its origin as well as in its commission. As
many readers may never have seen the
inside of a printing office, the following
short explanation may be found useful :
A 'case' is a shallow wooden drawer,
divided into numerous square receptacles
called 'boxes,' and into each box is put
one sort of letter only, say all *a*'s, or *b*'s,
or *c*'s. The compositor works with two of
these cases slanting up in front of him,
and when, from a shake, a slip, or any
other accident, the letters become mis-
placed the result is technically known as
' a foul case.' A further result is, that the
fingers of the workman, although going to
the proper box, will often pick up a wrong
letter, he being entirely unconscious the
while of the fact.

" Now, if we can discover any law which
governs this abnormal position of the types
—if, for instance, we can predicate that the
letter *o*, when away from its own, will be
more frequently found in the box appro-
priated to letter *a* than any other ; that *b*

has a general tendency to visit the l box, and l the v box; and that d, if away from home, will be almost certainly found among the n's; if we can show this, we shall then lay a good foundation for the re-examination of many corrupt or disputed readings in the text of Shakspere, some of which may receive fresh life from such a treatment.

"To start with, let us obtain a definite idea of the arrangement of the types in both 'upper' and 'lower' case in the time of Shakspere—a time when long s's, with the logotypes *ct, ff, fi, ffi, ffl, sb, sh, si, sl, ss, ssi, ssl,* and others, were in daily use."

Mr. Blades then refers to Moxon's *Mechanical Exercises,* 1683, which contains a representation of the compositors' cases in the seventeenth century, which may be presumed to be the same in form as those used in Shakespeare's day. Various alterations have been made in the arrangement of the cases, with the object of placing the letters more conveniently. The present form is shown on pp. 110, 111.

Mr. Blades proceeds : " The chief cause of a 'foul' case was the same in Shakspere's time as now ; and no one interested in the subject should omit visiting a printing office, where he could personally inspect the operation. Suppose a compositor at work 'distributing'; the upper and lower cases, one above the other, slant at a considerable angle towards him, and as the types fall quickly from his fingers they form conical heaps in their respective boxes, spreading out in a manner very similar to the sand in the lower half of an hour-glass. Now, if the compositor allows his case to become too full, the topmost letters in each box will certainly slide down into the box below, and occasionally, though rarely, into one of the side boxes. When such letters escape notice, they necessarily cause erroneous spelling, and sometimes entirely change the whole meaning of a sentence. But now comes the important question : Are errors of this kind ever discovered, and especially do they occur in Shakspere ? Doubtless they do, but to what extent a long and careful examination alone can

G	F	E	D	C	B	A	†	§	û	ó	í	é	å
O	N	M	L	K	I	H	+	=	ù	ò	ì	è	à
W	V	T	S	R	Q	P	*	¶	û	ô	î	é	â
J	U	Œ	Æ	Z	Y	X	J	U	Œ	Æ	Z	Y	X
G	F	E	D	C	B	A	ſ	ʒ	ü	ö	ï	ĕ	ä
O	N	M	L	K	I	H	7	6	5	4	3	2	1
W	V	T	S	R	Q	P	k	¾	½	¼	0	9	8

LOWER CASE.

fl	ff	fi	Em quads.		Large quads.
Leaders.	Leaders.	Leaders.	En quads.		
;	g		w	..	
!	f		,	q	.
?	s		·p	r	
( )			y		
Thin and middling spaces.	i		o	a	
	e		h	Thick spaces.	
'	d		n	t	
j					
æ œ	c		m	u	
[ ]	b		l	v	
&	|	ffl	ffi	Hair spaces.	z	x

show.   As examples merely, and to show the possible change in sense made by a single wrong letter, I will quote one or two instances :—

> ' Were they not *forc'd* with those that should
>   be ours,
>   We might have met them darefull, beard to
>   beard.'
>
> Macbeth, v. 5.[1]

The word *forced* should be read *farced,* the letter *o* having evidently dropped down into *a* box.   The enemy's ranks were not *forced* with Macbeth's followers, but *farced* or filled up.   In Murrell's *Cookery,* 1632, this identical word is used several times ; we there see that a farced leg of mutton was when the meat was all taken out of the skin, mixed with herbs, etc., and then the skin filled up again.

> ' I come to thee for charitable license . . .
>   To booke our dead.'
>
> Henry V., iv. 7.

So all the copies, but ' to book ' is surely a modern commercial phrase, and the

---

[1] Collier's MS. corrector substituted *farc'd* for *forc'd.*

Herald here asked leave simply to ' look,'
or to examine, the dead for the purpose
of giving honourable burial to their men
of rank.   In the same sense Sir W. Lucie,
in the First Part of *Henry VI.*, says :—

'I come to know what prisoners thou hast tane,
     And to survey the bodies of the dead.'

We cannot imagine an officer with pen,
inkhorn, and paper, at a period when few
could write, ' booking ' the dead.   We
may, I think, take it for granted that here
the letter *b* had fallen over into the *l*
box."

Another point to bear in mind is the
existence of such logotypes as *fi*, *si*, etc.,
so that, as Mr. Blades says, " the change of
light into sight must not be considered as
a question of a single letter—of *s* in the
l box," because the box containing *si* is
far away from the *l* box, and their contents could not well get mixed.

To these instances given by Mr. Blades
may be added a very interesting correction
suggested to the author some years ago
by a Shakespearian student.   When Isa-
bella visits her brother in prison, the

cowardly Claudio breaks forth in com-
plaint, and paints a vivid picture of the
horrors of the damned :—

" Ay, but to die, and go we know not where ;
　To lie in cold obstruction, and to rot ;
　This sensible warm motion to become
　A kneaded clod ; and the *delighted spirit*
　To bathe in fiery floods, or to reside
　In thrilling regions of thick-ribbed ice ;
　To be imprisoned in the viewless winds,
　And blown with restless violence round about
　The pendent world ; or to be worse than worst
　Of those that lawless and incertain thoughts
　Imagine howling !—'tis too horrible !
　The weariest and most loathed worldly life
　That age, ache, penury, and imprisonment
　Can lay on nature, is a paradise
　To what we fear of death."
　　　　　Measure for Measure, act iii., sc. 1.

We have here, in the expression "delighted spirit," a difficulty which none of
the commentators have as yet been able
to explain.   Warburton said that the
adjective meant "accustomed to ease
and delights," but this was not a very
successful guess, although Steevens
adopted it.   Sir Thomas Hanmer altered
delighted to *dilated*, and Dr. Johnson

mentions two suggested emendations, one being *benighted* and the other *delinquent.* None of these suggestions can be corroborated by a reference to the plans of the printers' cases, but it will be seen that the one now proposed is much strengthened by the position of the boxes in those plans. The suggested word is *deleted*, which accurately describes the spirits as destroyed, or blotted out of existence. The word is common in the printing office, and it was often used in literature.

If we think only of the recognised spelling of the word *delighted* we shall find that there are three letters to alter, but if we take the older spelling, *delited*, the change is very easily made, for it will be noticed that the letters in the *i* box might easily tumble over into the *e* box.

There is a very curious description of hell in Bede's *Ecclesiastical History*, where the author speaks of "deformed spirits" who leap from excess of heat to cutting cold, and it is not improbable that Shakespeare may have had this passage in his

mind when he put these words into the
mouth of Claudio.[1]

It is taken for granted that the compositor is not likely to put his hand into
the wrong box, so that if a wrong letter
is used, it must have fallen out of its
place.

An important class of misprints owes
its origin to this misplacement; but, as
noticed by Mr. Blades, there are other
classes, such as misspellings caused by
the compositor's ignorance or misunderstanding. We must remember that the
printer has to work fast, and if he does
not recognise a word he is very likely to
turn it into something he does understand. Thus the title of a paper in the
Philosophical Transactions was curiously
changed in an advertisement, and the
Calamites, a species of fossil plants of
the coal measures, with but slight change
appeared as "The True Fructification of
Calamities." This is a blunder pretty sure
to be made, and within a few days of
writing this, the author has seen a refer-

[1] An article on this point will be found in *The
Antiquary*, vol. viii. (1883), p. 200.

ence to "Notes on some Pennsylvanian
Calamities." As an instance of less excusable ignorance, we shall often find the
word *gauge* printed as *guage*.

One of the slightest of misprints was
the cause of an odd query in the second
series of *Notes and Queries*, which, by the
way, has never yet been answered. In
John Hall's *Horæ Vacivæ* (1646) there is
this passage, alluding to the table game
called *tick-tack.* The author wrote:
"Tick tack sets a man's intentions on
their guard. Errors in this and war can
be but once amended"; but the printer
joined the two words "and war" into one,
and this puzzled the correspondent of
the *Notes and Queries* (v. 272). He
asked : "Who can quote another passage
from any author containing this word?
I have hunted after it in many dictionaries without avail. It means, I suppose,
antagonism or contest, and resembles in
form many Anglo-Saxon words which
never found their way into English proper."
The blunder was not discovered, and
another correspondent wrote: "The word
andwar would surely modernise into *hand-*

war. Is not andirons (handirons) a parallel word of the same genus?" In the General Index we find "Andwar, an old English word." So much for the long life of a very small blunder.

A very similar blunder to this of "andwar" occurs in *Select Remains of the learned John Ray with his Life by the late William Derham,* which was published in 1760 with a dedication to the Earl of Macclesfield, President of the Royal Society, signed by George Scott. In Derham's Life of Ray a list of books read by Ray in 1667 is printed from a letter to Dr. Lister, and one of these is printed "The Business about great Rakes." Mr. Scott must have been puzzled with this title; but he was evidently a man not to be daunted by a difficulty, for he added a note to this effect : " They are now come into general use among the farmers, and are called *drag rakes.*" Who would suspect after this that the title is merely a misprint, and that the pamphlet refers to the proceedings of Valentine Greatrakes, the famous stroker, who claimed equal power with the kings and queens of England in curing the king's evil ? This blunder will be found uncorrected in Dr. Lankester's *Memorials of John Ray*, published by the Ray Society in 1846, and does not seem to have been suspected until the Rev. Richard Hooper called attention to it a short time ago in *Notes and Queries*.[1]

An amusing instance of the invention of a new word was afforded when the printer produced the words " a noticeable fact in thisms " instead of " this MS."

The misplacement of a stop, or the transposition of a letter, or the dropping out of one, will make sad havoc of the sense of a passage, as when we read of the *immoral* works of Milton. It was, however, a very complimentary misprint by which it was made to appear that a certain town had a remarkably high rate of *morality*. In the address to Dr. Watts by J. Standen prefixed to that author's *Horæ Lyricæ* (Leeds, 1788) this same misprint occurs, to the serious confusion of Mr. Standen's meaning,—

---

[1] Seventh Series, iv. 225.

" With thought sublime
And high sonorous words, thou sweetly sing'st
To thy *immoral* lyre."

On another page of this same book Watts' " daring flight " is transposed to *darling flight*.

In Miss Yonge's *Dynevor Terrace* a portion of one word was joined on to another with the awkward result that a young lady is described " without stretched arms."

The odd results of the misplacement of stops must be familiar to most readers ; but it is not often that they are so serious as in the following instances. William Sharp, the celebrated line engraver, believed in the Divine mission of the madman Richard Brothers, and engraved a portrait of that worthy with the following inscription beneath it : " Fully believing this to be the man appointed by God, I engrave his likeness.—W. SHARP." The writing engraver by mistake put the comma after the word *appointed*, and omitted it at the latter part of the sentence, thus giving a ludicrous effect to the whole inscription. Many impressions were struck off before the mistake was discovered and rectified. The question of an apostrophe was the ground of a civil action a few years ago in Switzerland ; and although the anecdote refers to a manuscript, and not to a printed document, it is inserted here because it illustrates the subject. A gentleman left a will which ended thus : " Et pour témoigner à mes neveux Charles et Henri de M——— toute mon affection je lègue à chacun *d'eux* cent mille francs." The paper upon which the will was written was folded up before the ink was dry, and therefore many of the letters were blotted. The legatees asserted that the apostrophe was a blot, and therefore claimed two instead of one hundred thousand francs each.

Several misprints are always recurring, such as the mixture of the words Topography and Typography, and Biography with Bibliography. In the prospectus of an edition of the *Waverley Novels* we read : " The aim of the publishers has been to make it pre-eminent, by beauty of *topography* and illustration, as an *édition de luxe.*"

Andrew Marvell published a book which

he entitled *The Rehearsal Transprosed*; but it is seldom that a printer can be induced to print the title otherwise than as *The Rehearsal Transposed.*

It must be conceded in favour of printers that some authors do write an execrable hand. One sometimes receives a letter which requires about three readings before it can be understood. At the first time of reading the meaning is scarcely intelligible, at the second time some faint glimpse of the writer's object in writing is obtained, and at the third time the main point of the letter is deciphered. Such men may be deemed to be the plague of printers. A friend of Beloe "the Sexagenarian" was remonstrated with by a printer for being the cause of a large amount of swearing in his office. "Sir," exclaimed Mr. A., "the moment 'copy' from you is divided among the compositors, volley succeeds volley as rapidly and as loudly as in one of Lord Nelson's victories."

There is a popular notion among authors that it is not wise to write a clear hand ; and Ménage was one of the first to express it. He wrote : " If you desire that no mistakes shall appear in the works which you publish, never send well-written copy to the printer, for in that case the manuscript is given to young apprentices, who make a thousand errors ; while, on the other hand, that which is difficult to read is dealt with by the master-printers." It is also related that the late eminent Arabic scholar, Mr. E. W. Lane, who wrote a particularly good hand, asked his printer how it was that there were always so many errors in his proofs. He was answered that such clear writing was always given to the boys, as experienced compositors could not be spared for it. The late Dean Hook held to this opinion, for when he was asked to allow a sermon to be copied out neatly for the press, he answered that if it were to be printed he would prefer to write it out himself as badly as he could. This practice, if it ever existed, we are told by experienced printers does not exist now.

It must, one would think, have been the badness of the " copy " that induced the compositors to turn " the nature and theory of the Greek verb " into *the native theology of the Greek verb* ; " the conservation of energy " into *the conversation of energy* ; and the " Forest Conservancy Branch " into the *Forest Conservatory Branch.*

Some printers go out of their way to make blunders when they are unable to understand their " copy." Thus, in the *Times*, some years ago, among the contributors to the Garibaldi Fund was a bookbinder who gave five shillings. The next down in the list was one " A. Lega Fletcher," a name which was printed as *A Ledger stitcher.*

Some very extraordinary blunders have been made by the ignorant misreading of an author's contractions. It is said that in a certain paper which was sent to be printed the words Indian Government were contracted as Indian Govt. This one compositor set up throughout his turn as *Indian goat.* A writer in one of the Reviews wrote the words " J. C. first invaded Britain," and a worthy compositor, who made it his business to fill up all the abbreviations, printed this as *Jesus Christ* instead of Julius Cæsar.

Here it may be remarked that some of

the most extraordinary misprints never get farther than the printing office or the study ; but although they may have been discovered by the reader or the author, they were made nevertheless.

Sometimes the fun of a misprint consists in its elaborateness and completeness, and sometimes in its simplicity (perhaps only the change of a letter). Of the first class the transformation of Shirley's well-known lines is a good example :—

> " Only the actions of the just
> Smell sweet and blossom in the dust "

is scarcely recognisable as

> " All the low actions of the just
> Swell out and blow Sam in the dust."

The statement that "men should work and play Loo," obtained from " men should work and play too," illustrates the second class.

The version of Pope which was quoted by a correspondent of the *Times* about a year ago is very charming :—

> " A little learning is a dangerous thing ;
> Drink deep, or aste not the aperient spring."

The reporter or printer who mistook the Oxford professor's allusion to the Eumenides, and quoted him as speaking of "those terrible old Greek goddesses—the Humanities," was still more elaborate in his joke.

Horace Greeley is well known to have been an exceedingly bad writer ; but when he quoted the well-known line (which is said to be equal to a florin, because there are four tizzies in it)—

"'Tis true, 'tis pity, pity 'tis 'tis true,"

one might have expected the compositor to recognise the quotation, instead of printing the astonishing calculation—

" 'Tis two, 'tis fifty and fifty 'tis, 'tis five."

This is as bad as the blunder of the printer of the Hampshire paper who is said to have announced that Sir Robert Peel and a party of *fiends* were engaged shooting *peasants* at Drayton Manor.

It is perhaps scarcely fair to quote too many blunders from newspapers, which must often be hurriedly compiled, but naturally they furnish the richest crop.

The point of a leader in an American paper was lost by a misprint, which reads as follows : " We do battle without shot or charge for the cause of the right." This would be a very ineffectual battle, and the proper words were *without stint or change.*

A writer on Holland in one of the magazines quoted Samuel Butler's well-known lines—

"A country that draws fifty foot of water,

.   .   .   .

In which they do not live, but go aboard,"

which the printer transformed into

" In which they do not live, but *cows abound.*"

It is of course easy to invent misprints, and therefore one feels a little doubtful sometimes with respect to those which are quoted without chapter and verse.

One of the most remarkable blunders ever made in a newspaper was connected with the burial of the well-known literary man, John Payne Collier. In the *Standard* of Sept. 21st, 1883, it was reported that "the remains of the late Mr. John Payne Collier were interred yesterday in Bray Churchyard, near Maidenhead, in the presence of a large number of spectators." The paragraph maker of the *Eastern Daily Press* had never heard of Payne Collier, so he thought the last name should be printed with a small C, and wanting a heading for his paragraph he invented one straight off, and this is what appeared in that paper :—

"*The Bray Colliery Disaster.* The remains of the late John Payne, collier, were interred yesterday afternoon in the Bray Churchyard, in the presence of a large number of friends and spectators."

This was a brilliant stroke of imagination, for who would expect to find a colliery near Maidenhead ?

Mr. Sala, writing to *Notes and Queries* (Third Series, i. 365), says : " Altogether I have long since arrived at the conclusion that there are more ' devils ' in a printing office than are dreamt of in our philosophy—the blunder fiends to wit—ever busy in peppering the ' formes ' with errors which defy the minutest revisions of reader, author, sub-editor, and editor." Mr. Sala gives an instance which occurred to himself. He wrote that Dr. Livingstone wore a cap with a tarnished gold lace band; but the printer altered the word tarnished into *famished*, to the serious confusion of the passage.

Some of the most amusing blunders occur by the change of a single letter. Thus, in an account of the danger to an express train by a cow getting on the line in front, the reporter was made to say that as the safest course under the circumstances the engine driver "put on full steam, dashed up against the cow, and literally cut it into *calves.*" A short time ago an account was given in an address of the early struggles of an eminent portrait painter, and the statement appeared in print that, working at the easel from eight o'clock in the morning till eight o'clock at night, the artist "only lay down on the hearthrug for rest and refreshment between the visits of his *sisters.*" This is not so bad, however, as the report that "a bride was accompanied to the altar by *tight* bridesmaids." A very odd blunder occurred in the *World* of Oct. 6th, 1886, one which was so odd that the editor

9

thought it worthy of notice by himself in a subsequent number. The paragraph in which the misprint occurred related to the filling up of the vicarage of St. Mary's, Islington, which it was thought had been unduly delayed. The trustees in whose gift the living is were informed that if they had a difficulty in finding a clergyman of the proper complexion of low churchism there were still Venns in Kent. Here the natural confusion of the letters *u* and *n* came into play, and as the paragraph was printed it appeared that a *Venus* of Kent was recommended for the vicarage of St. Mary's.

The compositor who set up the account of a public welcome to a famous orator must have been fresh from the study of Porson's *Catechism of the Swinish Multitude* when he set up the damaging statement that "the crowd rent the air with their *snouts.*"

Sometimes the blunder consists not in the misprint of a letter, but in a mere transposition, as when an eminent herald and antiquary was dubbed *Rogue Croix* instead of *Rouge Croix*. Sometimes a

new but appropriate word results by the
thrusting into a˙ recognised word of a re-
dundant letter, as when a man died from
eating too much goose the verdict was
said to have been "death from stuffoca-
tion."

Many of these blunders, although amusing to the public, cannot have been altogether agreeable to the subjects of them.
Mr. Justice Wightman could not have
been pleased to see himself described
as *Mr. Justice Nightman* ; and the right
reverend prelate who was stated "to be
highly pleased with some ecclesiastical
iniquities shown to him" must have been
considerably scandalised.

Professor Hales is very much of the
opinion of Mr. Sala respecting the labours
of the "blunder fiend," and he sent an
amusing letter to the *Athenæum*, in which
he pointed out a curious misprint in one
of his own books. As the contents of the
letter is very much to the point, readers
will perhaps not object to seeing it trans-
ferred in its entirety to these pages :—

"The humour of compositors is apt to be
imperfectly appreciated by authors, because

it rather interferes with what the author
wishes to say, although it may often say
something better.   But there is no reason
why the general reader should not
thoroughly enjoy it.   Certainly it ought to
be more generously recognised than it is.
So many persons at present think of it
as merely accidental and fortuitous, as if
there was no mind in it, as if all the excellent things loosely described as *errata*, all
the *curiosæ felicitates* of the setter-up of
texts, were casual blunders.   Such a view
reminds one of the way in which the last-
century critics used to speak of Shakspere
—the critics who give him no credit for
design or selection, but thought that some-
how or other he stumbled into greatness.
However, I propose now not to attempt
the defence, or, what might be worth the
effort, the analysis of this species of wit,
but only to give what seemed an admir-
able instance of it.

" In a note to the word *limboes* in the
Clarendon Press edition of Milton's
Areopagitica, I quoted from Nares's Glos-
sary a list of the various *limbi* believed
in by the ' old schoolmen,' and No. 2

was 'a *limbus patrum* where the fathers
of the Church, saints, and martyrs, awaited
the general resurrection.' Will any one
say it was not a stroke of genius in some
printing-office humourist to alter the last
word into '*in*surrection'?

"Like all good wit, this change is so
suggestive. It raises up a cloud of new
ideas, and reduces the hearer to a delightful confusion. How strangely it revises
all our popular notions! If even beyond
the grave the great problems that keep
men here restless and murmuring are not
solved! If even there the rebellious spirit
is not quieted! Nay, if those whom we
think of as having won peace for themselves in this world, do in that join the
malcontents, and are each one biding their
time—

ὡς τὴν Διὸς τυραννίδ' ἐκπέρσων βίᾳ.

"May we not conceive this bold jester,
if haply he were a stonemason, chiselling
on some tombstone '*In*surgam'?"

Allusion has already been made to the
persistency of misprints and the difficulty
of curing them; but one of the most

curious instances of this may be found in a line of Byron's beautiful apostrophe to the ocean in *Childe Harold* (Canto iv.). The one hundred and eighty-second stanza is usually printed :—

> "Thy shores are empires, changed in all save thee—
> Assyria, Greece, Rome, Carthage, what are they ?
> Thy waters wasted them while they were free,
> And many a tyrant since . . ."

Not many years ago a critic, asking himself the question when the waters wasted these countries, began to suspect a misprint, and on consulting the manuscript, it was found that he was right. The blunder, which had escaped Byron's own eyes, was corrected, and the third line was printed as originally written :—

> "Thy waters wash'd them power while they were free."

The carelessness of printers seems to have culminated in their production of the Scriptures. The old editions of the Bible swarm with blunders, and some of them were supposed to have been made intentionally. It was said that the printer

Field received £1500 from the Independents as a bribe to corrupt a text which might sanction their practice of lay-ordination, and in Acts vi. 3 the word *ye* is substituted for *we* in several of his editions of the Bible. The verse reads : " Wherefore, brethren, look ye out among ye seven men of honest report, full of the Holy Ghost and wisdom, whom *ye* may appoint over this business." To such forgeries Butler refers in the lines :—

> " Religion spawn'd a various rout
> Of petulant capricious sects,
> The maggots of corrupted texts."
> *Hudibras*, Part III., Canto 2.

Dr. Grey, in his notes on this passage, brings forward the charge against Field, and quotes Wotton's Visitation Sermon (1706) in support of it. He also quotes from Cowley's *Puritan and Papist* as to the practice of corrupting texts :—

> " They a bold pow'r o'er sacred Scriptures take,
> Blot out some clauses and some new ones make."

Pope Sixtus the Fifth's Vulgate so swarmed with errors that paper had to

be pasted over some of the erroneous
passages, and the public naturally laughed
at the bull prefixed to the first volume
which excommunicated any printer who
altered the text. This was all the more
annoying to the Pope, as he had intended
the edition to be specially free from errors,
and to attain that end had seen all the
proofs himself. Some years ago a copy
of this book was sold in France for 1210
francs.

The King's Printers, Robert Barker and
Martin Lucas, in the reign of Charles I.
were not excommunicated, but, what perhaps they liked less, were fined £300
by the Court of High Commission for
leaving the *not* out of the seventh commandment in an edition of the Bible
printed in 1631. Although this story has
been frequently quoted it has been dis-
believed, and the great bibliographer of
Bibles, the late Mr. George Offer, asserted
that he and his father searched diligently
for it, and could not find it. Now, six
copies are known to exist. The late Mr.
Henry Stevens gives a most interesting
account of the first discovery of the book

in his *Recollections of Mr. James Lennox.*
He writes :—

" Mr. Lennox was so strict an observer of the Sabbath that I never knew of his writing a business letter on Sunday but once. In 1855, while he was staying at Hotel Meurice in Paris, there occurred to me the opportunity one Saturday afternoon, June 16th, of identifying the long lost octavo Bible of 1631 with the negative omitted in the seventh commandment, and purchasing it for fifty guineas. No other copy was then known, and the possessor required an immediate answer. However, I raised some points of inquiry, and obtained permission to hold the little sinner and give the answer on Monday. By that evening's post I wrote to Mr. Lennox, and pressed for an immediate reply, suggesting that this prodigal though he returned on Sunday should be bound. Monday brought a letter ' to buy it,' very short, but tender as a fatted calf. On June 21st I exhibited it at a full meeting of the Society of Antiquaries of London, at the same time nicknaming it *The Wicked Bible,* a name that stuck to

it ever since, though six copies are now
known. . . . Lord Macaulay was present
at the meeting, but did not at first credit
the genuineness of the typographical
error.   Lord Stanhope, however, on
borrowing the volume, convinced him
that it was the true wicked error."

Curiously enough, when Mr. Stevens
took the Bible home on Saturday night
he overhauled his pile of octavo Bibles,
and found an imperfect duplicate of the
supposed unique "wicked" Bible.   When
the owner came for his book on Monday
morning he was shown the duplicate, and
agreed, as his copy was not unique, to
take £25 for it.   The imperfect copy
was sold to the British Museum for
eighteen guineas, and Mr. Winter Jones
was actually so fortunate as to obtain
subsequently the missing twenty-three
leaves.   A third copy came into the
hands of Mr. Francis Fry, of Bristol,
who sold it to Dr. Bandinel for the
Bodleian Library.   A fourth copy is in
the Euing Library, at Glasgow; a fifth
fell into the hands of Mr. Henry J.
Atkinson, of Gunnersbury, in 1883; and

a sixth copy was picked up in Ireland by a gentleman of Coventry in 1884.

In a Bible of 1634 the first verse of the 14th Psalm is printed as "The fool hath said in his heart there is God"; and in another Bible of 1653 *worldly* takes the place of *godly*, and reads, "In order that all the world should esteem the means of arriving at worldly riches."

If Field was not a knave, as hinted above, he was singularly unfortunate in his blunders; for in another of his Bibles he also omitted the negative in an important passage, and printed 1 Corinthians vi. 9 as, "Know ye not that the unrighteous shall inherit the kingdom of God?"

It is recorded that a printer's widow in Germany once tampered with the purity of the text of a Bible printed in her house, for which crime she was burned to death. She arose in the night, when all the workmen were in bed, and going to the "forme" entirely changed the meaning of a text which particularly offended her. The text was Gen. iii. 16 ("Thy desire shall be to thy husband, and he shall rule over thee").

This story does not rest on a very firm foundation, and as the recorder does not mention the date of the occurrence, it must be taken by the reader for what it is worth. The following incident, vouched for by a well-known author, is, however, very similar. James Silk Buckingham relates the following curious anecdote in his *Autobiography* :—

" While working at the Clarendon Printing Office a story was current among the men, and generally believed to be authentic, to the following effect. Some of the gay young students of the University, who loved a practical joke, had made themselves sufficiently familiar with the manner in which the types are fixed in certain formes and laid on the press, and with the mode of opening such formes for correction when required ; and when the sheet containing the Marriage Service was about to be worked off, as finally corrected, they unlocked the forme, took out a single letter *v*, and substituted in its place the letter *k*, thus converting the word *live* into *like*. The result was that, when the sheets were printed, that part of the service which rendered the bond irrevocable, was so changed as to make it easily dissolved—as the altered passage now read as follows :—The minister asking the bridegroom, ' Wilt thou have this woman to be thy wedded wife, to live together after God's ordinance in the holy state of matrimony ? Wilt thou love her, comfort her, honour, and keep her in sickness and in health ; and forsaking all other, keep thee only unto her, so long as ye both shall *like* ? ' To which the man shall answer, ' I will.' The same change was made in the question put to the bride."

If the culprits who left out a word deserved to be heavily mulcted in damages, it is difficult to calculate the liability of those who left out whole verses. When Archbishop Ussher was hastening to preach at Paul's Cross, he went into a shop to purchase a Bible, and on turning over the pages for his text found it was omitted.

Andrew Anderson, a careless, faulty printer in Edinburgh, obtained a monopoly as king's printer, which was exercised on

his death in 1679 by his widow. The
productions of her press became worse
and worse, and her Bibles were a standing disgrace to the country. Robert
Chambers, in his *Domestic Annals of
Scotland,* quotes the following specimen
from an edition of 1705 : " Whyshouldit-
bethougtathingincredi ble w^t you, y^t
God should raise the dead ? "   Even this
miserable blundering could not have been
much worse than the Pearl Bible with
six thousand errata mentioned by Isaac
Disraeli.

The first edition of the English Scriptures printed in Ireland was published at
Belfast in 1716, and is notorious for an
error in Isaiah. *Sin no more* is printed
Sin on more. In the following year was
published at Oxford the well-known
Vinegar Bible, which takes its name from
a blunder in the running title of the
twentieth chapter of St. Luke's Gospel,
where it reads " The parable of the
vinegar," instead of " The parable of the
vineyard."   In a Cambridge Prayer Book
of 1778 the thirtieth verse of Psalm cv. is
travestied as follows : " Their land brought

forth frogs, yea *seven* in their king's
chambers." An Oxford Bible of 1792
names St. Philip instead of St. Peter as
the disciple who should deny Christ
(Luke xxii. 34); and in an Oxford New
Testament of. 1864 we read, "Rejoice,
and be exceeding *clad*" (Matt. v. 12).
To be impartial, however, it is necessary
to mention a Cambridge Bible of 1831,
where Psalm cxix. 93 appears as "I will
never *forgive* thy precepts." A Bible
printed at Edinburgh in 1823 contains a
curious misprint caused by a likeness in
pronunciation of two words, Esther being
printed for Easter, "Intending after
Esther to bring him forth to the people"
(Acts xii. 4). A misprint of the old
hundredth Psalm (*do well* for *do dwell*) in
the Prayer Book might perhaps be considered as an improvement,—

"All people who on earth do well."

Errors are specially frequent in figures,
often caused by the way in which the
characters are cut. The aim of the
founder seems to be to make them as
much alike as possible, so that it fre-

quently requires a keen eye to discover the difference between a 3 and a 5. In one of Chernac's *Mathematical Tables* a line fell out before going to press, and instead of being replaced at the bottom of the page it was put in at the top, thus causing twenty-six errors. Besides these, however, only ten errors have been found in the whole work of 1020 pages, all full of figures. Vieta's *Canon Mathematicus* (1579) is of great rarity, from the author being discontented with the misprints that had escaped his notice, and on that account withdrawing or repurchasing all the copies he could meet with. Some mathematicians, to ensure accuracy, have made their calculations with the types in their own hands. In the *Imperial Dictionary of Universal Biography* there is a misprint in a date which confuses a whole article. William Ayrton, musical critic, is said to have been born in London about 1781, but curiously enough his father is reported to have been born three years afterwards (1784); and still more odd, that father was appointed gentleman of the Chapel Royal in 1764, twenty years before he is stated to have been born.

In connection with figures may be mentioned the terrible confusion which is caused by the simple dropping out of a decimal point. Thus a passage in which 6·36 is referred to naturally becomes utter nonsense when 636 is printed instead. Such a misprint is as bad as the blunder of the French compositor, who, having to set up a passage referring to Captain Cook, turned *de Cook* into *de* 600 *kilos.* An amusing blunder was quoted a few years ago from a German paper where the writer, referring to Prince Bismarck's endeavours to keep on good terms with all the Powers, was made to say, "Prince Bismarck is trying to keep up honest and straightforward relations *with all the girls.*" This blunder was caused by the substitution of the word Mädchen (girls) for Mächten (powers).

The French have always been interested in misprints, and they have registered a considerable number. One of the happiest is that one which was caused by Malherbe's bad writing, and induced him to

adopt the misprint in his verse in place
of that which he had originally written.
The lines, written on a daughter of Du
Perrier named Rosette, now stand thus :—

" Mais elle était du monde où les plus belles choses
    Ont le pire destin,
  Et rose, elle a vécu ce que vivent les roses
  L'espace d'un matin."

Malherbe had written,—

  " Et Rosette a vécu ce que vivent les roses ; "

but forgetting "to cross his tees" the
compositor made the fortunate blunder
of printing *rose elle*, which so pleased the
author that he let it stand, and modified
the following lines in accordance with the
printer's improvement.

Rabelais nearly got into trouble by
a blunder of his printer, who in several
places set up *asne* for *âme*. A council
met at the Sorbonne to consider the
case against him, and the doctors for-
mally denounced Rabelais to Francis I.,
and requested permission to prosecute
him for heresy ; but the king after consideration refused to give the permission.

Rabelais then laughed at his accusers for founding a charge of heresy against him on a printer's blunder, but there were strong suspicions that the misprints were intentional.

These misprints are styled by the French *coquilles*, a word whose derivation M. Boutney, author of *Dictionnaire de l'Argot des Typographes*, is unable to explain after twenty years' search. A number of *Longman's Magazine* contains an article on these *coquilles*, in which very many amusing blunders are quoted. One of these gave rise to a pun which is so excellent that it is impossible to resist the temptation of transferring the anecdote from those pages to these :—

" In the Rue Richelieu there is a statue of Corneille holding a roll in his hand, on which are inscribed the titles of his principal works. The task of incising these names it appears had been given to an illiterate young apprentice, who thought proper to spell *avare* with two r's. A wit, observing this, remarked pleasantly, *Tiens, voilà un avare qui a un air misanthrope* (un r mis en trop)."

In a newspaper account of Mr. Gladstone's religious views the word *Anglican* is travestied as *Afghan*, with the following curious result : " There is no form of faith in existence more effectually tenacious than the *Afghan* form, which asserts the full catholicity of that branch church whose charter is the English Church Prayer Book."

In the diary of John Hunter, of Craigcrook, it is recorded that at one of the meetings between the diarist, Leigh Hunt, and Carlyle, " Hunt gave us some capital specimens of absurd errors of the press committed by printers from his copy. One very good one occurs in a paper, where he had said, ' he had a liking for coffee because it always reminded him of the *Arabian Nights*,' though not mentioned there, adding, ' as smoking does for the same reason.' This was converted into the following oracular words : ' As sucking does for the snow season ' ! He could not find it in his heart to correct this, and thus it stands as a theme for the profound speculations of the commentators."

A very slight misprint will make a great difference ; sometimes an unintelligible word is produced, but sometimes the mere transposition of a letter will make a word exactly opposite in its meaning to the original, as *unite* for *untie*. In Jeremy Taylor's *XXV. Sermons preached at Golden Grove: Being for the Winter Half-year* (London, 1653), p. 247, we read, "It may help to unite the charm," whereas the author wished to say "untie."

The title of Cobbett's *Horse-hoeing Husbandry* was easily turned into *Horse-shoeing Husbandry*, that of the *Holy Grail* into *Holy Gruel*, and Layamon's *Brut* into Layamon's *Brat*.

A local paper, reporting the proceedings at the Bath meeting of the British Association, affirmed that an eminent chemist had "not been able to find any *fluidity* in the Bath waters." *Fluorine* was meant. It was also stated that a geologist asserted that "the bones found in the submerged forests of Devonshire were closely representative of the British *farmer*." The last word should have been *fauna*.

The strife of *tongs* is suggestive of a more serious battle than that of talk only; and the compositor who set up Portia's speech—

> ". . . young Alcides, when he did redeem
> The virgin tribute paid by howling Troy"
> (*Merchant of Venice*, act iii., sc. 2),

and turned the last words into *howling Tory*, must have been a rabid politician.

The transposition of "He kissed her under the silent stars" into "He kicked her under the cellar stairs" looks rather too good to be true, and it cannot be vouched for; but the title "Microscopic Character of the Virtuous Rocks of Montana" is a genuine misprint for *vitreous*, as is also "Buddha's perfect *uselessness*" for "Buddha's perfect sinlessness." It is rather startling to find a quotation from the *Essay on Man* introduced by the words "as the Pope says," or to find the famous painter Old Crome styled an "old Crone."

A most amusing instance of a mis-reading may be mentioned here, although it is not a literary blunder. A certain black cat was named Mephistopheles, a name which greatly puzzled the little girl who played with the cat, so she very sensibly set to work to reduce the name to a form which she could understand, and she arrived at "Miss Pack-of-fleas."

Sometimes a ludicrous blunder may be made by the mere closing up of two words ; thus the orator who spoke of our "grand Mother Church" had his remark turned into a joke when it 'was printed as "grandmother Church." A still worse blunder was made in an obituary notice of a well-known congressman in an American paper, where the reference to his "gentle, manly spirit" was turned into "gentlemanly spirit."

Misprints are very irritating to most authors, but some can afford to make fun of the trouble ; thus Hood's amusing lines are probably founded upon some blunder that actually occurred :—

> " But it is frightful to think
> What nonsense sometimes
> They make of one's sense,
> And what's worse, of one's rhymes.

" It was only last week,
   In my ode upon Spring,
Which I meant to have made
   A most beautiful thing,

" When I talked of the dew-drops
   From freshly-blown roses,
The nasty things made it
   From freshly-blown noses.

" And again, when, to please
   An old aunt, I had tried
To commemorate some saint
   Of her clique who had died,

" I said he had taken up
   In heaven his position,
And they put it—he'd taken
   Up to heaven his *physician*."

Henry Stephens (Estienne), the learned
printer, made a joke over a misprint. The
word *febris* was printed with the diphthong
æ, so Stephens excused himself by saying
in the errata that " le chalcographe a fait
une fièvre longue (fœbrem) quoique une
fièvre courte (febrem) soit moins dan-
gereux."

Allusion has already been made in the
first chapter to Professor Skeat's ghost

words. Most of these have arisen from misreadings or misprints, and two extraordinary instances may be noted here. The purely modern phrase "look sharp" was supposed to have been used in the time of Chaucer, because "loke schappe" (see that you form, etc.) of the manuscript was printed "loke scharpe." In the other instance the scribe wrote *yn* for *m*, and thus he turned "chek matyde" into "chek yn a tyde."[1]

In the *Academy* for Feb. 25th, 1888, Dr. Skeat explained another discovery of his of the same kind, by which he is able to correct a time-honoured blunder in English literature :—

"CAMBRIDGE : *Feb.* 14, 1888.

"When I explained, in the *Academy* for January 7 (p. 9), that the word 'Herenus' is simply a mistake for 'Herines,' *i.e.*, the furies (such being the Middle-English form of Erinnyes), I did not expect that I should so soon light upon another singular perversion of the same word.

[1] *Philol. Soc. Trans.*, 1885-7, pp. 368-9.

"In Chaucer's Works, ed. 1561, fol. 322, back, there is a miserable poem, of much later date than that of Chaucer's death, entitled 'The Remedie of Love.' The twelfth stanza begins thus:

' Come hither, thou Hermes, and ye furies all
  Which fer been under us, nigh the nether pole,
  Where Pluto reigneth,' etc.

It is clear that 'Hermes' is a scribal error for 'Herines,' and that the scribe has added 'thou' out of his own head, to keep 'Hermes' company. The context bears this out; for the author utterly rejects the inspiration of the Muses in the preceding stanza, and proceeds to invoke furies, harpies, and, to use his own expression, 'all this lothsome sort.' Many of the lines almost defy scansion, so that no help is to be got from observing the run of the lines. Nevertheless, this fresh instance of the occurrence of 'Herines' much assists my argument; all the more so, as it appears in a disguised shape.

                    "WALTER W. SKEAT."

Sometimes a misprint is intentional, as

in the following instance. At the beginning of the century the *Courrier des Pays
Bas* was bought by some young men, who
changed its politics, but kept on the editor.
The motto of the paper was from Horace :

" Est modus in rebus,"

and the editor, wishing to let his friends
at a distance know that things were not
going on quite well between him and his
proprietors, printed this motto as,—

" Est nodus in rebus."

This was continued for three weeks before
it was discovered and corrected by the
persons concerned.

Another kind of misprint which we see
occasionally is the misplacement of some
lines of type. This may easily occur when
the formes are being locked, and the result
is naturally nonsense that much confuses
the reader. Probably the finest instance of
this misplacement occurred some years ago
in an edition of *Men of the Time* (1856),
where the entry relating to Samuel Wilber-
force, Bishop of Oxford, got mixed up
with that of Robert Owen, the Socialist,

with the result that the bishop was stated to be "a confirmed sceptic as regards revealed religion, but a believer in Spiritualism." It was this kind of blunder which suggested the formation of cross-readings, that were once very popular.

CHAPTER VII.

Schoolboys' Blunders.

THE blunders of the examined form a fruitful source of amusement for us all, and many comical instances have been published. The mistakes which are constantly occurring must naturally be innumerable, but only a few of them rise to the dignity of a blunder. If it be difficult to define a blunder, probably the best illustration of what it is will be found in the answers of the boys under examination. All classes of blunders may be found among these. There are those which show confusion of knowledge, and those which exhibit an insight into the heart of the matter while blundering in the form. Two very good examples occur to one's mind, but it is to be feared that they owe their origin to some keen spirit of mature years. " What is Faith ?—The quality by which we are enabled to believe that which we know is untrue." Surely this must have emanated from a wit! Again, the whole Homeric question is condensed into the following answer : " Some people say that the Homeric poems were not written by Homer, but by another man of the same name." If this is a blunder, who would not wish to blunder so?

A large class of schoolboys' blunders consist in a confusion of words somewhat alike in sound, a confusion that is apt to follow some of us through life. " Matins " has been mixed up with " pattens," and described as something to wear on the feet. Nonconformists are said to be persons who cannot form anything, and a tartan is assumed to be an inhabitant of Tartary. The gods are believed by one boy to live on nectarines, and by another to imbibe ammonia. The same desire to make an unintelligible word express a meaning which has caused the recognised but absurd spelling of *sovereign* (more wisely spelt *sovran* by Milton) shows itself in the form " Tea-trarck "

explained as the title of Herod given to
him because he invented or was fond of
tea.[1] A still finer confusion of ideas is to
be found in an answer reported by Miss
Graham in the *University Correspondent*:
"Esau was a man who wrote fables, and
who sold the copyright to a publisher for
a bottle of potash."

The following etymological guesses are
not so good, but they are worthy of regis-
tration. One boy described a blackguard
as "one who has been a shoeblack," while
another thought he was "a man dressed
in black." "Polite" is said to be derived
from "Pole," owing to the affability of the
Polish race. "Heathen" means "covered
with heath"; but this explanation is
commonplace when compared with the
brilliant guess—"Heathen, from Latin
'hæthum,' faith, and 'en,' not."

The boy who explained the meaning of
the words *fort* and *fortress* must have had
rather vague ideas as to masculine and
feminine nouns. He wrote: "A fort is
a place to put men in, and a fortress a
place to put women in."

[1] *Cornhill Magazine*, June 1888, pp. 619-28.

The little book entitled *English as she is Taught*, which contains a considerable number of genuine answers to examination questions given in American schools, with a Commentary by Mark Twain, is full of amusing matter. A large proportion of these answers are of a similar character to those just enumerated, blunders which have arisen from a confusion caused by similarity of sound in the various words, thus, " In Austria the principal occupation is gathering Austrich feathers." The boy who propounded this evidently had much of the stock in trade required for the popular etymologist. " Ireland is called the Emigrant Isle because it is so beautiful and green." " Gorilla warfare was where men rode on gorillas." " The Puritans found an insane asylum in the wilds of America."

Some of the answers are so funny that it is almost impossible to guess at the train of thought which elicited them, as, " Climate lasts all the time, and weather only a few days." " Sanscrit is not used so much as it used to be, as it went out of use 1500 B.C." The boy who affirmed that "The imports of a country are the things that are paid for ; the exports are the things that are not," did not put the Theory of Exchange in very clear form.

The knowledge of physiology and of medical subjects exhibited by some of the examined is very amusing. One boy discovered a new organ of the body called a chrone : " He had a chronic disease— something the matter with the chrone." Another had a strange notion of how to spell *craniology*, for he wrote " Chonology is the science of the brane." But best of all is the knowledge of the origin of Bright's disease, shown by the boy who affirms that " John Bright is noted for an incurable disease."

Much of the blundering of the examined must be traced to the absurd questions of the examiners—questions which, as Mark Twain says, " would oversize nearly anybody's knowledge." And the wish which every examinee has to bring in some subject which he supposes himself to know is perceptible in many answers. The date 1492 seems to be impressed upon every American child's memory, and he cannot rest until he has associated it with some fact, so we learn that George Washington was born in 1492, that St. Bartholomew was massacred in that year, that "the Brittains were the Saxons who entered England in 1492 under Julius Cæsar," and, to cap all, that the earth is 1492 miles in circumference.

Many of the best-known examination jokes are associated with Scriptural characters. One of the best of these, if also one of the best known, is that of the man who, paraphrasing the parable of the Good Samaritan, and quoting his words to the innkeeper, "When I come again I will repay you," added, "This he said knowing that he should see his face again no more."

A School Board boy, competing for one of the Peek prizes, carried this confusion of widely different events even farther. He had to write a short biography of Jonah, and he produced the following: "He was the father of Lot, and had two wives. One was called Ishmale and the other Hagher; he kept one at home, and he turned the other into the dessert, when

she became a pillow of salt in the daytime
and a pillow of fire at night." The sketch
of Moses is equally unhistoric : " Mosses
was an Egyptian. He lived in an ark
made of bullrushes, and he kept a golden
calf and worshipped braizen snakes, and
et nothing but kwales and manna for forty
years. He was caught by the hair of his
head, while riding under the bough of a
tree, and he was killed by his son Absalom
as he was hanging from the bough." But
the ignorance of the schoolboy was quite
equalled by the undergraduate who was
asked "Who was the first king of Israel?"
and was so fortunate as to stumble on
the name of Saul. Finding by the face
of the examiner that he had hit upon
the right answer, he added confidentially,
" Saul, also called Paul."

The American child, however, managed
to cover a larger space of time in his confusion when he said, " Elijah was a good
man, who went up to heaven without
dying, and threw his cloak down for
Queen Elizabeth to step over."

A boy was asked in an examination,
" What did Moses do with the tabernacle?"

and he promptly answered, " He chucked it out of the camp." The scandalised examiner asked the boy what he meant, and was told that it was so stated in the Bible. On being challenged for the verse, the boy at once repeated " And Moses took the tabernacle and *pitched* it without the camp" (Exod. xxxiii. 7).

The book might be filled with extraordinary instances of school translation, but room must be found for one beautiful specimen quoted by Moore in his *Diary.* A boy having to translate "they ascended by ladders" into Latin, turned out this, " ascendebant per adolescentiores " (the comparative degree of lad, *i.e.,* ladder).

The late Mr. Barrett, Musical Examiner to the Society of Arts, gave some curious instances of blundering in his report on the Examinations of 1887, which is printed in the *Programme of the Society's Examinations for* 1888 :—

" There were occasional indications that the terms were misunderstood. ' Presto ' signifies ' turn over,' ' Lento ' ' with style.' ' Staccato ' was said to mean ' stick on the notes,' or 'notes struck and at once raised.' . . .

"The names of composers in order of time were generally correctly done, but the particulars concerning the musicians were rather startling. Thus Purcell was said to have written, among other things, an opera called *Ebdon and Eneas*; one stated that he was born 1543 and died 1595, probably confusing him with Tallis, that he wrote masses and reformed the church music; another that he was the organist of King's College Chapel, and wrote madrigals. One stated that he was born 1568 and died 1695; another, not knowing that he had so long passed the allotted period of man's existence, gave his dates 1693, 1685, thus giving him no limit of existence at all. One said he was a German, born somewhere in the nineteenth century, which statement another confirmed by giving his dates as 1817—1846; and, further, credited him with the composition of *The Woman of Samaria*, and as having transposed plain-song from tenor to bass. Bach is said to have been the founder of the 'Thames

School Lipsic,' the composer of the *Seasons*, the celebrated writer of opera comique, born 16—, and having gone through an operation for one of his fingers, turned his attention to composition, wrote operas, and, lastly, that he was born in 1756, and died 1880, and that his fame rests on his passions.

"The facts about Handel are pretty correct; but we find that Weber wrote *Parsifal, The Flying Dutchman, Der Ring der Nibulengon.* His dates are 1813—1883. Mendelssohn was born 1770, died 1827 (Beethoven's dates), studied under Hadyn (*sic*), and that he composed many operas. Gounod is said to be 'a rather modern musician'; he wrote *Othello, Three Holy Children*, besides *Faust* and other works. Among the names given as the composer of *Nozze di Figaro* are Donizetti, William Sterndale Bennett, Gunod, and Sir Mickall Costa.   The particulars concerning the real composer are equally interesting. (1) His name is spelt Mozzart, Mosarde, etc. (2) He was a well-known Italian, wrote *Medea*, and others. (3) His first opera was *Idumea*, or *Idomeo*.   (4) He composed

Lieder ohne worte, Don Pasquale, Don Govianna, the *Zauberfloat, Feuges,* and his *Requiem* is the crowning glory of his 'marvellious carere.' (5) He was a German, 'born 1756, at a very early age.' If the dates given by another writer be true (born 1795, died 1659), it is certain that he must have died before he was born."

Mr. Barrett again reported in 1889 some of the strange opinions of those who came to him to be examined :—

"The answers to the question 'Who was Rossini? What influence did he exercise over the art of music in his time?' brought to light much curious and interesting intelligence. His nationality was various. He was 'a German by birth, but was born at Pesaro in Italy'; 'he was born in 1670 and died 1826'; he was a 'Frenchman,' 'a noted writer of the French,' the place of nativity was 'Pizzarro in Genoa'; he was 'an Italian, and made people feel drunk with the sparke and richness of his melody'; he composed *Oberon, Don Giovanni, Der Frieschutz,* and *Stabet Matar.* He was 'an accom-

plished writer of violin music and produced some of the prettiest melodies';
it is 'to him we owe the extension of
chords struck together in ar peggio'; he
was 'the founder of some institution or
another'; 'the great aim of his life was
to make the music he wrote an interpretation of the words it was set to'; he
'broke many of the laws of music'; he
'considerable altered the stage'; he
'was noted for using many instruments
not invented before'; in his 'composition he used the chromatic scale very
much, and goes very deep in harmony';
he 'was the first taking up the style, and
therefore to make a great change in
music'; he was 'the cause of much censure and bickering through his writings';
he 'promoted a less strict mode of writing
and other beneficial things'; and, finally,
'Giachono Rossini was born at Pezarro
in 1792.   In the year 1774 there was war
raging in Paris between the Gluckists and
Piccinists.   Gluck wanted to do away with
the old restraint of the Italian aria, and
improve opera from a dramatic point of
view.   Piccini remained true to the old

Italian style, and Rossini helped him to carry it on still further by his operas, *Tancredi*, *William Tell*, and *Dorma del Lago*.'"

The child who gave the following brilliant answer to the question, " What was the character of Queen Mary?" must have suffered herself from the troubles supposed to be connected with the possession of a stepmother : " She was wilful as a girl and cruel as a woman, but" (adds the pupil) "what can you expect from any one who had had five stepmothers?"

The greatest confusion among the examined is usually to be found in the answers to historical and geographical questions. All that one boy knew about Nelson was that he "was buried in St. Paul's Cathedral amid the groans of a dying nation." The student who mixed up Oliver Cromwell with Thomas Cromwell's master Wolsey produced this strange answer : " Oliver Cromwell is said to have exclaimed, as he lay a-dying, If I had served my God as I served my king, He would not have left me to mine enemies." Miss Graham relates in the *University*

Correspondent an answer which contains the same confusion with a further one added : " Wolsey was a famous general who fought in the Crimean War, and who, after being decapitated several times, said to Cromwell, Ah ! if I had only served you as you have served me, I would not have been deserted in my old age."

" The Spanish Armada," wrote a young man of seventeen, " took place in the reign of Queen Anne ; she married Philip of Spain, who was a very cruel man. The Spanish and the English fought very bravely against each other. The English wanted to conquer Spain. Several battles were fought, in which hundreds of the English and Spanish were defeated. They lost some very large ships, and were at a great loss on both sides."

The following description of the Nile by a schoolboy is very fine : " The Nile is the only remarkable river in the world. It was discovered by Dr. Livingstone, and it rises in Mungo Park." Constantinople is described thus : " It is on the Golden Horn ; a strong fortress ; has a University, and is the residence of Peter the Great.

Its chief building is the Sublime Port."
Amongst the additions to our geographical
knowledge may be mentioned that Gibraltar is "an island built on a rock," and
that Portugal can only be reached through
the St. Bernard's Pass "by means of
sledges drawn by reindeer and dogs."
"Turin is the capital of China," and
"Cuba is a town in Africa very difficult
of access."

One of the finest answers ever given in
an examination was that of the boy who
was asked to repeat all he knew of Sir
Walter Raleigh. This was it: "He introduced tobacco into England, and while
he was smoking he exclaimed, 'Master
Ridley, we have this day lighted such a
fire in England as shall never be put
out.'" Can that, with any sort of justice,
be styled a blunder?

The rule that "the King can do no
wrong" was carried to an extreme length
when a schoolboy blunder of Louis XIV.
was allowed to change the gender of
a French noun. The King said "un
carosse," and that is what it is now.
In Cotgrave's *Dictionary carosse* appears

as feminine, but Ménage notes it as having been changed from feminine to masculine.

It has already been pointed out that some of the blunders of the examined are due to the absurdity of the questions of the examiner. The following excellent anecdote from the late Archdeacon Sinclair's *Sketches of Old Times and Distant Places* (1875) shows that even when the question is sound a difficulty may arise by the manner of presenting it :—

"I was one day conversing with Dr. Williams about schools and school examinations. He said : ' Let me give you a curious example of an examination at which I was present in Aberdeen. An English clergyman and a Lowland Scotsman visited one of the best parish schools in that city. They were strangers, but the master received them civilly, and inquired : "Would you prefer that I should *speer* these boys, or that you should *speer* them yourselves?" The English clergyman having ascertained that to *speer* meant to question, desired the master to proceed. He did so with great success, and the boys answered numerous interrogatories as to the Exodus from Egypt. The clergyman then said he would be glad in his turn to *speer* the boys, and began : " How did Pharaoh die ? " There was a dead silence. In this dilemma the Lowland gentleman interposed. " I think, sir, the boys are not accustomed to your English accent," and inquired in broad Scotch, " Hoo did Phawraoh dee ? " Again there was a dead silence, till the master said : " I think, gentlemen, you can't *speer* these boys ; I'll show you how." And he proceeded : " Fat cam to Phawraoh at his hinder end ? " *i.e.,* in his latter days. The boys with one voice answered, " He was drooned " ; and a smart little fellow added, " Ony lassie could hae told you that." The master then explained that in the Aberdeen dialect "to dee " means to die a natural death, or to die in bed : hence the perplexity of the boys, who knew that Pharaoh's end was very different.' "

The author is able to add to this chapter a thoroughly original series of answers to certain questions relating to acoustics, light and heat, which Professor Oliver

Lodge, F.R.S., has been so kind as to communicate for this work, and which cannot fail to be appreciated by his readers. It must be understood that all these answers are genuine, although they are not given *verbatim et literatim*, and in some instances one answer is made to contain several blunders. Professor Lodge expresses the opinion that the questions might in some instances have been worded better, so as to exclude several of the misapprehensions, and therefore that the answers may be of some service to future setters of questions. He adds that of late the South Kensington papers have become more drearily correct and monotonous, because the style of instruction now available affords less play to exuberant fancy untrammelled by any information regarding the subject in hand.

1880.—ACOUSTICS, LIGHT AND HEAT
PAPER.
Science and Art Department.

The following are specimens of answers given by candidates at recent examinations in Acoustics, Light and Heat, held in connection with the Science and Art Department, South Kensington. The answers have not of course all been selected from the same paper, neither have they all been chosen for the same reason.

Question 1.—State the relations existing between the pressure, temperature, and density of a given gas. How is it proved that when a gas expands its temperature is diminished?

Answer.—Now the answer to the first part of this question is, that the square root of the pressure increases, the square root of the density decreases, and the absolute temperature remains about the same; but as to the last part of the question about a gas expanding when its temperature is diminished, I expect I am intended to say I don't believe a word of it, for a bladder in front of a fire expands, but its temperature is not at all diminished.

Question 2.— If you walk on a dry path between two walls a few feet apart, you hear a musical note or "ring" at each footstep. Whence comes this?

Answer.—This is similar to phospho-rescent paint. Once any sound gets between two parallel reflectors or walls, it bounds from one to the other and never stops for a long time. Hence it is persistent, and when you walk between the walls you hear the sounds made by those who walked there before you. By following a muffin man down the passage within a short time you can hear most distinctly a musical note, or, as it is more properly termed in the question, a "ring" at every (other) step.

Question 3.—What is the reason that the hammers which strike the strings of a pianoforte are made not to strike the middle of the strings? Why are the bass strings loaded with coils of wire?

Answer.—Because the tint of the clang would be bad. Because to jockey them heavily.

Question 4.—Explain how to determine the time of vibration of a *given* tuning-fork, and state what apparatus you would require for the purpose.

Answer.—For this determination I should require an accurate watch beating seconds, and a sensitive ear. I mount the fork on a suitable stand, and then, as the second hand of my watch passes the figure 60 on the dial, I draw the bow neatly across one of its prongs. I wait. I listen intently. The throbbing air particles are receiving the pulsations; the beating prongs are giving up their original force; and slowly yet surely the sound dies away. Still I can hear it, but faintly and with close attention; and now only by pressing the bones of my head against its prongs. Finally the last trace disappears. I look at the time and leave the room, having determined the time of vibration of the common "pitch" fork. This process deteriorates the fork considerably, hence a different operation must be performed on a fork which is only *lent*.

Question 6.—What is the difference between a "real" and a "virtual" image? Give a drawing showing the formation of one of each kind.

Answer.—You see a real image every morning when you shave. You do not see virtual images at all. The only people who see virtual images are those people

who are not quite right, like Mrs. A.
Virtual images are things which don't
exist.   I can't give you a reliable drawing
of a virtual image, because I never saw
one.

Question 8.—How would you disprove,
experimentally, the assertion that white
light passing through a piece of coloured
glass acquires colour from the glass ? What
is it that really happens ?

Answer.—To disprove the assertion (so
repeatedly made) that " white light passing
through a piece of coloured glass acquires
colour from the glass," I would ask the
gentleman to observe that the glass has
just as much colour after the light has
gone through it as it had before.   That is
what would really happen.

Question 11.—Explain why, in order to
cook food by boiling, at the top of a high
mountain, you must employ a different
method from that used at the sea level.

Answer.—It is easy to cook food at the
sea level by boiling it, but once you get
above the sea level the only plan is to fry
it in its own fat.   It is, in fact, impossible
to boil water above the sea level by any

amount of heat. A different method, therefore, would have to be employed to boil food at the top of a high mountain, but what that method is has not yet been discovered. The future may reveal it to a daring experimentalist.

Question 12.—State what are the conditions favourable for the formation of dew. Describe an instrument for determining the dew point, and the method of using it.

Answer.—This is easily proved from question 1. A body of gas as it ascends expands, cools, and deposits moisture ; so if you walk up a hill the body of gas inside you expands, gives its heat to you, and deposits its moisture in the form of dew or common sweat. Hence these are the favourable conditions ; and moreover it explains why you get warm by ascending a hill, in opposition to the well-known law of the Conservation of Energy.

Question 13.—On freezing water in a glass tube, the tube sometimes breaks. Why is this ? An iceberg floats with 1,000,000 tons of ice above the water line. About how many tons are below the water line ?

Answer.—The water breaks the tube because of capallarity. The iceberg floats on the top because it is lighter, hence no tons are below the water line. Another reason is that an iceberg cannot exceed 1,000,000 tons in weight : hence if this much is above water, none is below. Ice is exceptional to all other bodies except bismuth. All other bodies have 1090 feet below the surface and 2 feet extra for every degree centigrade. If it were not for this, all fish would die, and the earth be held in an iron grip.

P.S.—When I say 1090 feet, I mean 1090 feet per second.

Question 14.—If you were to pour a pound of molten lead and a pound of molten iron, each at the temperature of its melting point, upon two blocks of ice, which would melt the most ice, and why?

Answer.—This question relates to diathermancy. Iron is said to be a diathermanous body (from *dia*, through, and *thermo*, I heat), meaning that it gets heated through and through, and accordingly contains a large quantity of real heat. Lead is said to be an athermanous body

(from *a*, privative, and *thermo*, I heat),
meaning that it gets heated secretly or in
a latent manner. Hence the answer to
this question depends on which will get
the best of it, the real heat of the iron or
the latent heat of the lead. Probably the
iron will smite furthest into the ice, as
molten iron is white and glowing, while
melted lead is dull.

Question 21.—A hollow indiarubber ball
full of air is suspended on one arm of a
balance and weighed in air. The whole
is then covered by the receiver of an air
pump. Explain what will happen as the
air in the receiver is exhausted.

Answer.—The ball would expand and
entirely fill the vessell, driving out all before
it. The balance being of greater density
than the rest would be the last to go, but
in the end its inertia would be overcome
and all would be expelled, and there would
be a perfect vacuum. The ball would
then burst, but you would not be aware of
the fact on account of the loudness of a
sound varying with the density of the place
in which it is generated, and not on that
in which it is heard.

Question 27.—Account for the delicate shades of colour sometimes seen on the inside of an oyster shell. State and explain the appearance presented when a beam of light falls upon a sheet of glass on which very fine equi-distant parallel lines have been scratched very close to one another.

Answer.—The delicate shades are due to putrefaction ; the colours always show best when the oyster has been a bad one. Hence they are considered a defect and are called chromatic aberration.

The scratches on the glass will arrange themselves in rings round the light, as any one may see at night in a tram car.

Question 29.—Show how the hypothenuse face of a right-angled prism may be used as a reflector. What connection is there between the refractive index of a medium and the angle at which an emergent ray is totally reflected ?

Answer.—Any face of any prism may be used as a reflector. The connexion between the refractive index of a medium and the angle at which an emergent ray does not emerge but is totally reflected is remarkable and not generally known.

Question 32.—Why do the inhabitants of cold climates eat fat ? How would you find experimentally the relative quantities of heat given off when equal weights of sulphur, phosphorus, and carbon are thoroughly burned ?

Answer.—An inhabitant of cold climates (called Frigid Zoans) eats fat principally because he can't get no lean, also because he wants to rise is temperature. But if equal weights of sulphur phosphorus and carbon are burned in his neighbourhood he will give off eating quite so much. The relative quantities of eat given off will depend upon how much sulphur etc. is burnt and how near it is burned to him. If I knew these facts it would be an easy sum to find the answer.

1881.

Question 1.—Sound is said to travel about four times as fast in water as in air. How has this been proved ? State your reasons for thinking whether sound travels faster or slower in oil than in water.

Answer (a).—Mr. Colladon, a gentleman
who happened to have a boat, wrote to a
friend called Mr. Sturm to borrow another
boat and row out on the other side of the
lake, first providing himself with a large
ear-trumpet. Mr. Colladon took a large
bell weighing some tons which he put
under water and hit furiously. Every time
he hit the bell he lit a fusee, and Mr.
Sturm looked at his watch. In this way
it was found out as in the question.

It was also done by Mr. Byott who sang
at one end of the water pipes of Paris,
and a friend at the other end (on whom he
could rely) heard the song as if it were a
chorus, part coming through the water and
part through the air.

(*b*) This is done by one person going into
a hall (? a well) and making a noise, and
another person stays outside and listens
where the sound comes from. When Miss
Beckwith saves life from drowning, her
brother makes a noise under water, and
she hearing the sound some time after can
calculate where he is and dives for him ;
and what Miss Beckwith can do under
water, of course a mathematician can do

on dry land. Hence this is how it is done.

If oil is poured on the water it checks the sound-waves and puts you out.

Question 2.—What would happen if two sound-waves exactly alike were to meet one another in the open air, moving in opposite directions?

Answer.—If the sound-waves which meet in the open air had not come from the same source they would not recognise each others existence, but if they had they would embrace and mutually hold fast, in other words, interfere with and destroy each other.

Question 9.—Describe any way in which the velocity of light has been measured.

Answer (*a*). — A distinguished but Heathen philosopher, Homer, was the first to discover this. He was standing one day at one side of the earth looking at Jupiter when he conjectured that he would take 16 minutes to get to the other side. This conjecture he then verified by careful experiment. Now the whole way across the earth is 3,072,000 miles, and dividing this by 16 we get the velocity 192,000 miles a second.   This is so great that it would take an express train 40 years to do it, and the bullet from a canon over 5000 years.

P.S.—I think the gentlemans name was Romer not Homer, but anyway he was 20% wrong and Mr. Fahrenheit and Mr. Celsius afterwards made more careful determinations.

(*b*) An Atheistic Scientist (falsely so called) tried experiments on the Satellites of Jupiter.   He found that he could delay the eclipse 16 minutes by going to the other side of the earths orbit ; in fact he found he could make the eclipse happen when he liked by simply shifting his position.   Finding that credit was given him for determining the velocity of light by this means he repeated it so often that the calendar began to get seriously wrong and there were riots, and Pope Gregory had to set things right.

Question 10.—Explain why water pipes burst in cold weather.

Answer.—People who have not studied

Acoustics think that Thor bursts the pipes, but we know that it is nothing of the kind for Professor Tyndall has burst the mythologies and has taught us that it is the natural behaviour of water (and bismuth) without which all fish would die and the earth be held in an iron grip.

CHAPTER VIII.

FOREIGNERS' ENGLISH.

T is not surprising that foreigners
should make mistakes when
writing in English, and Englishmen, who know their own deficiencies in
this respect, are not likely to be cen-
sorious when foreigners fall into these
blunders. But when information is printed
for the use of Englishmen, one would
think that the only wise plan was to have
the composition revised by one who is
thoroughly acquainted with the language.
That this natural precaution is not always
taken we have ample evidence. Thus, at
Havre, a polyglot announcement of certain
local regulations was posted in the harbour,
and the notice stood as follows in French :
" Un arrangement peut se faire avec le
pilote pour de promenades à rames." The
following very strange translation into

English appeared below the French:
"One arrangement can make himself
with the pilot for the walking with roars."

The papers distributed at international
exhibitions are often very oddly worded.
Thus, an agent in the French court of
one of these, who described himself as
an "Ancient Commercial Dealer," stated
on a handbill that "being appointed by
Tenants of the Exhibition to sell Show
Cases, Frames, &c., which this Court
incloses, I have the honour to inform
Museum Collectors, Librarians, Builders,
Shopkeepers, and business persons in
general, that the fixed prices will hardly be
the real value of the Glasses which adorn
them."

In 1864 was published in Paris a pre-
tentious work, consisting of notices of
the various literary and scientific societies
of the world, which positively swarms with
blunders in the portion devoted to England.
The new forms into which well-known
names are transmogrified must be seen to
be believed. Wadham College is printed
Washam, Warwick as *Worwick*; and one
of our metropolitan parks is said to be

dedicated to a saint whose name does not occur in any calendar, viz., *St. Jam's Park.* There is the old confusion respecting English titles which foreigners find so difficult to understand; and monsieur and esquire usually appear respectively before and after the names of the same persons. The Christian names of knights and baronets are omitted, so that we obtain such impossible forms as " Sir Brown."

The book is arranged geographically, and in all cases the English word " shire " is omitted, with the result that we come upon such an extremely curious monster as "le Comté de Shrop."

On the very first page is made the extraordinary blunder of turning the Cambrian Archæological Association into a *Cambridge* Society; while the Parker Society, whose publications were printed at the University Press, is entered under *Canterbury.* It is possible that the Latin name *Cantabrigia* has originated this mistake. The Roxburgh Society, although its foundation after the sale of the magnificent library of the Duke of Roxburgh is correctly described, is here placed under the county of Roxburgh. The most amusing blunder, however, in the whole book is contained in the following charmingly naïve piece of etymology *à propos* of the Geological and Polytechnic Society of the West Riding of Yorkshire : "On sait qu'en Anglais le mot *Ride* se traduit par voyage à cheval ou en voiture ; on pourrait peut-être penser, dès le début, qu'il s'agit d'une Société hippique. Il n'en est rien ; a l'exemple de l'Association Britannique, dont elle," etc. This pairs off well with the translation of *Walker, London,* given on a previous page.

The Germans find the same difficulty with English titles that the French do, and confuse the Sir at the commencement of our letters with Herr or Monsieur. Thus, they frequently address Englishmen as *Sir*, instead of mister or esquire. We have an instance of this in a publication of no less a learned body than the Royal Academy of Sciences of Munich, who issued in 1860 a " Rede auf Sir Thomas Babington Macaulay."

An hotel-keeper at Bale translated

"limonade gazeuse" as "gauze lemon-ads"; and the following delightful entry is from the Travellers' Book of the Drei Mohren Hotel at Augsburg, under date Jan. 28th, 1815 : "His Grace Arthur Wellesley, Duke of Wellington, &c., &c., &c. Great honour arrived at the begirming of this year to the three Moors. This illustrious warrior, whose glorious atchievements which cradled in Asia have filled Europe with his renown, descended in it." It may be thought that, as this is not printed, but only written, it is scarcely fair to preserve it here ; but it really is too good to leave out.

The keepers of hotels are great sinners in respect to the manner in which they murder the English language. The following are a few samples of this form of literature, and most readers will recall others that they have come across in their travels.

The first is from Salzburg :—

" George Nelböck begs leave to recommand his hotel to the Three Allied, situated *vis-a-vis* of the birth house of Mozart, which offers all comforts to the meanest charges."

The next notice comes from Rastadt :—

"ADVICE OF AN HOTEL.

"The underwritten has the honour of informing the publick that he has made the acquisition of the hotel to the Savage, well situated in the middle of this city. He shall endeavour to do all duties which gentlemen travellers can justly expect ; and invites them to please to convince themselves of it by their kind lodgings at his house.

"BASIL

"JA. SINGESEM.

"Before the tenant of the Hotel to the Stork in this city."

Whatever may be the ambition of mine host at Pompeii, it can scarcely be the fame of an English scholar :—

"Restorative Hotel Fine Hok,
Kept by Frank Prosperi,
Facing the military quarter
at Pompei.

That hotel open since a very few days is renowned for the cheapness of the Apart-

13

ments and linen, for the exactness of the
service, and for the excellence of the true
French cookery. Being situated at proxi-
mity of that regeneration, it will be propi-
tious to receive families, whatever, which
will desire to reside alternatively into that
town to visit the monuments now found
and to breathe thither the salubrity of the
air. That establishment will avoid to all
travellers, visitors of that sepult city and
to the artists (willing draw the antiquities)
a great disorder occasioned by tardy and
expensive contour of the iron whay people
will find equally thither a complete sort-
ment of stranger wines and of the kingdom,
hot and cold baths, stables, coach houses,
the whole at very moderated prices. Now
all the applications and endeavours of the
Hoste will tend always to correspond to
the tastes and desires of their customers
which will require without doubt to him
into that town the reputation whome, he
is ambitious."

On the occasion of the Universal Exhibition of Barcelona in 1888 the *Moniteur
de l'Exposition* printed a description of
Barcelona in French, German, Spanish,

and English. The latter is so good that it is worthy of being printed in full :—

" Then there will be in the same Barcelona the first universal Exposition of Spain. It was not possible to choose a more favorable place, for the capital-town of Catalonia is a first-rate city open to civilization.

" It is quite out of possibility to deny it to be the industrial and commercial capital of the peninsula and a universal Exposition could not possibly meet in any other place a more lively splendour than in this magnificent town.

" Indeed what may want Barcelona to deserve to be called great and handsome? Are here not to be found archeological and architectural riches, whose specimens are inexhaustible?

" What are then those churches whose style it is impossible to find elsewhere, containing altars embellished with truly spanish magnificence, and so large and imposing cloisters, that there feels any man himself exceedingly small and little? What those shaded promenades, where the sun cannot almost get through with the golden tinge of its rays? what this Rambla where every good citizen of Barcelona must take his walk at least once every day, in order to accomplish the civic pilgrimage of a true Catalanian?

"And that Paseo Colon, so picturesque with its palmtrees and electric light, which makes it like, in the evening, a theatrical decoration, and whose ornament has been very happily just finished?

"And that statue of Christopher Colomb, whose installation will be accomplished in a very short time, whose price may be 500,000 francs?

"Are not there still a number of proud buildings, richly ornamented, and splendid theaters? one of them, perhaps the most beautiful, surely the largest (it contains 5000 places) the Liceo, is truly a master-pièce, where the spectators are lost in admiration of the riches, the ornaments, the pictures and feel a true regret to turn their eyes from them to look at the stage.

"You will see coffee houses, where have been spent hundreds of thousands to change their large rooms in enchanted halls with which it would be difficult to contest even for the palaces of east.

" And still in those little streets, now very few, so narrow that the inhabitants of their opposite houses can shake hands together, do you not know that doors may be found which open to yards and staircases worthy of palaces?

" Do you not know there are plenty of sculptures, every one of them master-pieces, and that, especially the town and deputation house contain some halls which would make meditate all our great masters?

" If we walk through the Catalonia-square to reach the Ensanche, our astonishment becomes still greater.

" In this Ensanche, a newly-born, but already a great town, there are no streets : there are but promenades with trees on both sides, which not only moderate the rays of the sun through their follage, but purify the surrounding atmosphere and seem to say to those who are walking beneath their shade : You are breathing here the purest air!

" There display the houses plenty of

the rarest sorts of marble. Out and in-
doors rules marble, the ceilings of the
halls, the staircases, the yards command
and force admiration to the spectator,
who thought to see only houses and finds
monumental buildings.

"Join to that a Paseo de Gracia with
immense perspective ; the promenade of
Cortes, 10 kil. long ; some free squares
by day- and night-time, in which the rarest
plants and the sweetest flowers enchant
the passengers eyes and enbalm his
smell.

" Join lastly the neighbourhoods, but a
short way from the town and put on all
sides in communication with it by means
of tramways—lines and steam—tramways
too ; those places show a very charming
scenery for every one who likes natural
beauties mingled with those which are
created by the genius of man.

" After that all there is Monjuich, whose
proud fortress seems to say : I protect
Barcelona : half-way the slope of the
mountain, there are Miramar, Vista
Alegre, which afford one of the grandest
panorama in the world : on the left side,

the horizon skirting, some hills which
form a girdle, whose indented tops detach
them selves from an ever-blue sky ; at
the foot of those mountains, the suburbs
we have already mentioned, created for
the rest and enjoyment of man after his
accomplished duty and finished work ;
on the lowest skirt Barcelona in a flame
with its great buildings, steeples, towers,
houses ornamented with flat terraces, and
more than all that, its haven, which had
been, to say so, conquered over the
Mediterranean and harbors daily in itself
a large number of ships.

"All this ideal Whole is concentrated
beneath an enchanting sky, almost as
beautiful as the sky of Italy. The climate
of Barcelona is very much like Nice, the
pretty.

"Winter is here unknown ; in its place
there rules a spring, which allows every
plant to bud, every most delicate flower
to blossom, orangetrees and roses, throughout the whole year.

"In one word, Barcelona is a magnificent town, which is about to offer to the
world a splendid, universal Exposition,

whose success is quite out of doubt determined."

At the Paris Exhibition of 1889 a
Practical Guide was produced for the
benefit of the English visitor, which is
written throughout in the most astonishing jargon, as may be seen from the
opening sentences of the " Note of the
Editor," which run as follows : "The
Universal Exhibition, for whom who comes
there for the first time, is a true chaos
in which it is impossible to direct and
recognize one's self without a guide.
What wants the stranger, the visitor who
comes to the Exhibition, it is a means
which permits him to see all without
losing uselessly his time in the most part
vain researches."

This is the account of the first con-
ception of the Exhibition : "Who was
giving the idea of the Exhibition ? The
first idea of an Exhibition of the Cen-
tenary belongs in reality not to anybody.
It was in the air since several years, when
divers newspapers, in 1883, bethought
them to consecrate several articles to it,
and so it became a serious matter. The

period of incubation (brooding) lasted
since 1883 till the month of March 1884 ;
when they considered the question they
preoccupied them but about a National
Exhibition. Afterwards the ambition
increased. The ministery, then presided
by Mr. Jules Ferry, thought that if they
would give to this commercial and industrial manifestation an international character they would impose the peace not
only to France, but to the whole world."

The Eiffel Tower gives occasion for
some particularly fine writing : " In order
to attire the stranger, to create a great
attraction which assured the success of
the Exhibition, it wanted something exceptional, unrivalled, extraordinary. An
engineer presented him, Mr. Eiffel, already
known by his considerable and keen
works. He proposed to M. Locroy to
erect a tower in iron which, reaching the
height of three hundred metres, would
represent, at the industrial sight, the
resultant of the modern progresses. M.
Locroy reflected and accepted. Hardly
twenty years ago, this project would have
appeared fantastic and impossible. The

state of the science of the iron constructions was not advanced enough, the
security given by the calculations was not
yet assured; to-day, they know where
they are going, they are able to count the
force of the wind. The resistance which
the iron opposes to it. Mr. Eiffel came
at the proper time, and nevertheless how
many people have prophetized that the
tower would never been constructed.
How many critics have fallen upon this
audacious project! It was erected, however, and one perceives it from all Paris;
it astonishes and lets in extasy the strangers who come to contemplate it."

The figures attached to the fountain
under the tower are comically described
as follows:—

"Europe under the lines of a woman,
leaned upon a printing press to print and
a book, seems deeped in reflections.

"America is young woman, energetic and
virginal however, characterising the youth
and the audacies of the American people.

" Asia, the cradle of the human kind,
represents the volupty and the sensualism.
Her posture, the expression of her figure,

render well the abandonment of the passion with the oriental people.

" Africa represented by a figure of a woman in a timid attitude, is well the symbol of the savage people enslaved by the civilisation.

" Australia finally is figured by a woman buttressed on herself, like an animal not yet tamed, ready to throw itself on its prey, without waiting to be attacked. . . .

" Above Asia and Africa, the Love and the Sleep, in the shade of a floating drapery. Finally, between Europe and America, a young girl symbolises the History."

The author commences the account of his first walk as follows: " Thus we begin, at present as we have let him see these two wonderworks which fly at the eyes, the Tower and the fountain, to return on his steps to retake with order this walk of recognition which will permit him, thanks to our watchfulness, to see all in a short time."

"The History of the human dwelling" is introduced thus : " It is the moment or never to walk among the surprising

restitution, of which M. Garnier the
eminent architect of the Opera has made
him the promoter. On our left going
along the flower-beds from the Tower till
here, the constructions of the History of
the human Dwelling is unfolded to our
eyes. The human Dwelling in all countries and in all times, there is certainly
an excellent subject of study. Without
doubt the great works do not fail, where
conscientious plates enable us to know
exactly in which condition where living
our ancestors, how their dwellings where
disposed in the interior. But nothing
approaches the demonstration by the
materiality of the fact, and .it is struck
with this truth that the organisators of
the Exhibition resolved to erect an im-
provisated town, including houses of all
countries and all latitudes."

The author finishes up his little work
in the same self-satisfied manner, which
shows how unconscious he was that he
was writing rubbish :—

"There is finished our common walk,
and in a happy way, after six days which
we dare believe it did not seem to you

long, and tiresome, your curiosity finding a constant aliment at every step which we made you do, in this exhibition without rivalry, where the beauties succeed to the beauties, where one leaves not one pleasure but for a new one. As for us, our task of cicerone is too agreeable to us, that we shall do our best to retain you still near us, in efforcing us to discover still other spectacles, and to present you them after all those you know already."

If it be absurd to give information to Englishmen in a queer jargon which it is difficult for him to understand, what must be said of those who attempt to teach a language of which they are profoundly ignorant? Most of us can call to mind instances of exceedingly unidiomatic sentences which have been presented to our notice in foreign conversation books ; but certainly the most extraordinary of this class of blunders are to be found in the *New Guide of the Conversation in Portuguese and English*, by J. de Fonseca and P. Carolino, which created some stir in the English press a few years

ago.[1] The authors do not appear to
have had even the most distant acquaint-
ance with either the spoken or written
language, so that many of the sentences
are positively unintelligible, although
the origin of many of them may be
found in a literal translation of certain
French sentences. One chapter of this
wonderful book is devoted to *Idiotisms*,
which is a singularly appropriate title
for such odd English proverbs as the
following :—

"The necessity don't know the low."

"To build castles in Espaguish."

"So many go the jar to spring, than at
last rest there."

(A little further on we find another
version of this well-known proverb : "So
much go the jar to spring that at last it
break there.")

"The stone as roll not heap up not
foam."

"He is beggar as a church rat."

"To come back at their muttons."

---

[1] A selection from this book was printed by
Messrs. Field & Tuer under the title of *English
as she is spoke.*

"Tell me whom thou frequent, I will tell you which you are."

The apparently incomprehensible sentence "He sin in trouble water" is explained by the fact that the translator confused the two French words *pêcher*, to sin, and *pêcher*, to fish.

The classification adopted by the authors cannot be considered as very scientific. The only colours catalogued are *white, cray, gridelin, musk,* and *red*; the only "music's instruments"—*a flagelet, a dreum,* and *a hurdy-gurdy.* "Common stones" appear to be *loadstones, brick, white lead,* and *gumstone.* But probably the list of "Chastisements" is one of the funniest things in this Guide to Conversation. The list contains *a fine, honourable fine, to break upon, to tear off the flesh, to draw to four horses.*

The anecdotes chosen for the instruction of the unfortunate Portuguese youth are almost more unintelligible than the rest of the book, and probably the following two anecdotes could not be matched in any other printed book :—

"The Commander Forbin of Janson,

being at a repast with a celebrated
Boileau, had undertaken to pun upon
her name :—' What name, told him, carry
you thither ?   Boileau : I would wish
better to call me Drink wine.'   The poet
was answered him in the same tune :—
' And you, sir, what name have you choice ?
Janson : I should prefer to be named
John-meal.   The meal don't is valuable
better than the furfur.' "

The next is as good :—

" Plato walking one's self a day to the
field with some of their friends.   They
were to see him Diogenes who was in
water untill the chin.   The superficies
of the water was snowed, for the rescue
of the hole that Diogenes was made.
Don't look it more told them Plato, and
he shall get out soon."

A large volume entitled *Poluglôssos* was
published in Belgium in 1841, which is
even more misleading and unintelligible
than the Portuguese School Book.   The
English vocabulary contains some amazing
words, such as *agridulce, ales of troops,
ancientness sign, bivacq fire, breast's pellicule,
chimney black money, infatuated compass,*

jug (vocal), *window, umbrella,* etc. At the end of this vocabulary are these notes :—

" Look the abridged introduction exeptless for the english editions, foregoing the french postcript, next after the title page. Just as the numbers, the names of cities, states, seas, mountains and rivers, the christian names of men and woman, and several synonimous, who enter into the composition of many english words, suppressed in the former vocabulary, are explained by the respective categorys and appointed at the general index, look also by these, what is not found here above."

"*Version alternative.* See for the shorter introduction exeptless for the english editions, foregoing the french postscript next after the title page. Just as the numbers &c. . . . their expletives are be given by the respective categorys, and appointed at the general index, to wich is sent back ! "

We are frequently told that foreigners are much better educated than we are, and that the trade of the world is slipping

14

through our fingers because we are not
taught languages as the foreigners are.
This may be so, but one cannot help
believing that the dullest of English
clerks would be able to hold his own
in competition with the ingenious youths
who are taught foreign languages on the
system adopted by Senhors Fonseca
and Carolino, and by the compiler of
Poluglôssos.

Guides to a foreign town or country
written in English by a foreigner are
often very misleading; in fact, sometimes
quite incomprehensible. A contributor
to the *Notes and Queries* sent to . that
periodical some amusing extracts from a
Guide to Amsterdam. The following few
lines from a description of the Assize
Court give a fair idea of the language :—

"The forefront has a noble and sublime aspect, and is particularly character-
istical to what it ought to represent. It
is built in a division of three fronts in
the corinthic order, each of them consists
of four raising columns, resting upon a
general basement from the one end of
the forefront to the other, and supporting

a cornish, equalling running all over the
face." [1]

When it was known that Louis XVIII.
was to be restored to the throne of France,
a report was circulated that the Duke of
Clarence (afterwards William IV.) would
take the command of the vessel which was
to convey the king to Calais. The people
of that town were in a fever of expecta-
tion, and having decided to sing *God save
the King* in honour of their English visitor,
they thought that it would be an additional
compliment if they supplemented it with
an entirely new verse, which ran as
follows :—

" God save noble Clarénce,
　Who brings our King to France,
　　God save Clarénce ;
　He maintains the glorý
　Of the British navý,
　Oh God, make him happý,
　　God save Clarénce." [2]

In continuation of the story, it may be
said that the Duke did not go to Calais,

[1] *Notes and Queries*, First Series, iii. 347.
[2] *Ibid.*, iv. 131.

and that therefore the anthem was not sung.

The composer of this strange verse succeeded in making pretty fair English, even if his rhymes were somewhat deficient in correctness. This was not the case with a rather famous inscription made by a Frenchman. Monsieur Girardin, who inscribed a stone at Ermenonville in memory of our once famous poet Shenstone, was not stupid, but rather preternaturally clever. This inscription is above all praise for the remarkable manner in which the rhymes appeal to the eye instead of the ear ; and moreover it shows how world-famous was that charming garden at Leasowes, near Halesowen, which is now only remembered by the few :—

> " This plain stone
> To William Shenstone.
> In his writings he display'd
> A mind natural.
> At Leasowes he laid
> Arcadian greens rural."

Dr. Moore, having on a certain occasion excused himself to a Frenchman for using an expression which he feared was not French, received the reply, "Bon monsieur, mais il merite bien de l'être." Of these lines it is impossible to paraphrase this polite answer, for we cannot say that they deserve to be English.

INDEX.

216   *Index.*

Hugo's (Victor) translation, 50.
Hunt's (Leigh) specimens of misprints, 148.
Hyett s *Flowers from the South*, 74.

Ibn Roshd = Averrhoes, 54.
Immoral *for* immortal, 120.
Independent Whig, 53.
"Indifferent justice," 42.
Insurrection *for* resurrection, 133.

Jefferies (Judge) said to have presided at the trial
    of Charles I., 37.
Job's wish that his adversary had written a book,
    58.
Jonson's (Ben) *Every Man in his Humour*, 95.
Juvenal, edition of, with the first printed errata,
    78.

Lamartine's *Girondins*, translation of, 54.
Lamb's *Tales from Shakespeare*, 45.
Lane's (E. W.) good writing, 123.
La Rochefoucauld *as* Ruchfucove, 53.
Layamon's Brat *for* Brut, 149.
Le Berceau, an imaginary author, 67.
Leigh's (Edward) table of errata, 79.
Leviticus supposed to be a man, 17.
Leycester's (Sir Peter) *Historical Antiquities*, 97.
Littleton's Latin Dictionary, 10.
Lodge's (Prof. Oliver) series of examination papers,
    174.
Logotypes, 113.

For EU product safety concerns, contact us at Calle de José Abascal, 56–1°, 28003 Madrid, Spain or eugpsr@cambridge.org.

www.ingramcontent.com/pod-product-compliance
Ingram Content Group UK Ltd.
Pitfield, Milton Keynes, MK11 3LW, UK
UKHW010338140625
459647UK00010B/677